IN ALL THINGS
GOODNESS

Happy Birthday Alix

May the Goodness that abides
within bring you joy, peace & wisdom

Trudy

IN ALL THINGS GOODNESS

A Christian Vision for the 21st Century

GERTRUDE LEBANS

ABC Publishing
ANGLICAN BOOK CENTRE

2003
Anglican Book Centre
600 Jarvis Street
Toronto, Ontario
Canada M4Y 2J6

Most biblical quotations are adapted from the New Revised Standard Version of the Bible.

Text typeset in Palatino and Optima
Cover and text design by Jane Thornton

National Library of Canada Cataloguing in Publication

Lebans, Gertrude
    In all things goodness : a Christian vision for the 21st century / Gertrude Lebans.

Printed in Canada

ISBN 1-55126-361-0
1. Christianity. 2. Christian life. I. Title.

BR481.L42 2003   270.8'3   C2002-905724-8

CONTENTS

Introduction   7

In All Things, Goodness   11
In Change, Wisdom   41
In Suffering, Wholeness   63
In Repentance, Compassion   85
The Paradox of the Eternal   109
Spiritual Exercises   121

Endnotes   129

Introduction

fear and excitement have the same physiological origin
everything is in the interpretation

In the Anglican Church in our time, and in other denominations as well, we are facing multiple layers of crisis. We may choose to see these as opportunities or as threats, but even those of us who are resisting know that we are in a whirlwind and that everything is changing around us. I believe that this is a time of great potential. I believe that there is a polishing of the faith, in effect, and that we will see more clearly through the lens of Christianity when it is completed. I also believe that Christianity has a contribution to offer in the discussion of the meaning of life, but we need to formulate our conversation in ways that revisit some old ideas and take seriously the new knowledge that is unfolding in science and in biblical research.

Even to entertain some of the questions I have stirred up is problematic for many of us in the church; I myself am frightened sometimes when I preach or teach. I know, however, that although Jesus promised to be with us until the end, he also promised a cross, a sword, and a struggle for those who would follow him. I think this means that we must engage in creative and troubling conversations about what the faith has been and what it could become.

Since the time of Jesus, everything has changed. Most people know that the world is a round globe spinning in space. Buckminster Fuller commented once that there was no up or down in a curved universe.[1] Our theology, and much of our social organization, has been based on the cosmology of a flat world where up and down form the basis for reality. What does it mean to live in a round world where the only direction is around, where darkness and light are not opposites but complementary realities, where we know that neutrinos exist although they are invisible, where nano-millimeters can be measured, where life can be cloned and genetic modifications are routine? Our perception of our world and our biology is so very different that we would seem quite alien to the people of the first century.

I love the metaphors and narratives of the Bible, but I think we need to understand them and restate them in language and concepts that match what we know now. We need to learn how to separate an original "truth" from the cultural and scientific shielding that is conditioned by its context and place in history. To mistake mythology for history, metaphor for science, human truth for absolute truth, is to risk losing everything that is valuable in Christianity.[2] It seems to me that what the world needs is more willingness to listen, more openness to the inspiration of the Spirit, more opportunities for creative theology, more wonder, and, overall, less fearful control.

Our era is an era of faith, rather than belief. It is hard to know what to believe; faith, however, is a form of trust. We trust that God will not abandon us; we trust that each door of knowledge we unlock will have as much promise as danger. We trust that no matter how far we may stray, the Holy Spirit will guide us back to a "truer" vision of life.

This book is a doorway into some ways of thinking about what matters to us, how we adapt first-century metaphors and cosmology to a twenty-first-century consciousness. In the post-resurrection accounts of Jesus, his followers were told not to cling to him, not to stand staring into the blue sky, not to look back, but to move on down the road to heal, to forgive, and to rejoice. It is time for the church to move or be left behind, as the Spirit works in all of humanity to bring about a new day.

IN ALL THINGS, GOODNESS

looking in the mirror, i see myself
looking deeper, i see the light of Christ
deeper, i see the compassion of God
more deeply yet, i see the self
completed and whole

In the beginning, Being is always good, which is to say whole, holy, complete. For Jews and Christians, at the centre of all existence is this truth: Life is good. Sometimes we might be confused by this truth, because so much of what we have inherited about the faith says that life is, in fact, intrinsically and irredeemably "bad" without sacrificial redemption through Jesus the Christian Messiah. Indeed, some schools of Christian thinking maintain a doctrine that separates the saved — those who have accepted Jesus and, in some formulations, have led blameless lives — and the damned, who are everybody else. This dualistic thinking — good and bad, saved and damned — has a well-developed mythology for the emotionally vulnerable or the intellectually frozen, but little impact for mature thinkers. Nor is it satisfying for those who cannot accept the mythology and have no faith that the church has anything else to offer. Some of these latter folks — at least a generation away from any formal religious formation — do not even know how to begin to think about goodness or what it means to be alive.[3] The "scare" tactics of control, used by the Christian church, last only until there is opportunity to expand horizons or permission to disagree. For better or worse, many of these tactics have become the subject of parody and mockery.

Unfortunately, Christianity has been stereotyped as an "opiate" or as a way of deceiving the unwary. Historically, Christian differences have been remembered primarily as a history of violence and genocidal fanaticism. Our work in healing and education, our support of the poor and defence of the vulnerable, have been lost in the more dramatic stories of the Crusades, the Inquisitions, or the excesses of the Reformation era, for example. It is not surprising that few people would immediately suggest that goodness is the foundational principle of Christianity.

In this chapter, I hope to redeem this original understanding of goodness, not as behaviour, but as fundamental as DNA to the essential condition of being alive. I also hope that understanding goodness from a different perspective will facilitate some new ways of thinking about life and faith. To do this, I am going to examine the Genesis story, to show how Sabbath provides a spiritual model for experiencing goodness, and how we act from a conviction of goodness. Finally, I will briefly discuss evil as a social construction.

AND INDEED, IT WAS VERY GOOD

By goodness, I am suggesting something capable of being fulfilled, at least within human perception. Though it may appear partial, goodness has within itself the seeds of completion and maturity, or further transformation beyond the scope of our imaginations. Moreover, what is good is productive of an intentional and contained abundance.

> God saw everything that God had made, and indeed, it was very good.
> And there was evening and there was morning, the sixth day.
> [Genesis 1:31]

So goodness occurs when there is enough rain to grow crops on arable land, but not so much that there is flooding. Goodness is having enough to eat and some to share, but not so much that others are starving. Goodness is knowing when to say, "Enough," and when to say, "I need," and when to ask, "Do you need?" Goodness has a logical and observable discipline to it. If we poison our food supply, we will starve. Goodness says, "Let the earth and the water be healthy and clean."

Jesus says to his disciples, "Only God is good." Recognizing goodness, holiness, is naming the Divine in our lives. We say, "This is good," and we taste what is holy. We are saying that God is either whole and complete, or that God is capable of ongoing, persistent, and productive transformation. Original goodness is both the raw material and the work in progress, as it moves from the partial to the completion of a state of being. Goodness then is not a moral quality, but a quality of being. Goodness is the Alpha and the Omega, the beginning and the ending of what exists. Holiness is wholeness, completion, *teleios* in Greek — what rests within the Alpha and the Omega, yet surpasses the boundaries of creation and resolution. Goodness is the spark of holiness within the creation, the great variety of experience that reveals the holiness that imprints and surrounds the creation.

In what other ways can we capture this idea of goodness? If we use the metaphor of God as divine parent, the ultimate goodness as progenitor of all that is, then encoded within everything is a quality that is good — absolutely and indissolubly. By the idea of goodness, I do not mean perfection or flawlessness, but rather the indefinable elemental quality that allows us to glimpse what is complete or has an undiluted essence about it. We are not assigning some exterior grade to any thing or being, but rather discerning its intrinsic grace, truth, and beauty. And it is not simply grace, truth, or beauty by themselves, but the totality and unity to which we are responding. We resonate to some indefinable but recognizable quality that has the power to move us or charm us, to make us wonder or react in awe. This quality says either, "I am just at the beginning" and "I am just at my ending," or "I am the fullness that you call God." Goodness is the quality that we recognize as the unique, yet connected, nature of anything.

Frederick Buechner, in his book, *The Longing for Home*, speaks about a vision of wholeness that he experienced as a sign of the image of God within us. He tells of a visit that he and his family made to Sea World in Florida. There they watched the killer whale show.

> What with the dazzle of sky and sun, the beautiful young people on the platform, the soft southern air …. It was as if the whole creation — men and women and beasts and sun and water and earth and sky and, for all I know, God himself — was caught up in one great, jubilant dance of unimaginable beauty…. This is the joy that is so apt to be missing … the joy of not just imagining to believe at least part of the time that life is holy but of actually running into that holiness head-on…. I think maybe it is holiness that we long for more than we long for anything else.[4]

For those of us who believe that life is a mystery imbued

with the Divine, holiness can appear in the least likely places — a killer whale performance in Florida, the twinkle in a beggar's eye, the awesome display of the universe in the Northern Lights, the deadly beauty of a virus under the microscope, a bed of trout lilies found by chance in the woods, the devastation of the 1999 ice storm in Quebec and Ontario. And it is present in all the more usual places — great art, music, and literature; small children and wise seniors.

When I consider the incarnation of holiness, I can say that God is fully present in the minutiae of creation and also in the vastness beyond us, in the eternal past and in the infinite future. Perhaps God has even limited the divine freedom and is now tied to the unfolding of creation. I believe that God is invested in developing a relationship with all that is becoming. For Christians, the concept of Jesus' incarnation in the world signifies that God limits and links the Divineself within the Beloved, who incarnates the love of God and the best of humanity. If this is true for the nature of Jesus, then it is also true for all of us who, in the created order, share the DNA of the Holy One. We share in essential goodness, yet we have some freedom to explore the nature of our own existence.

When we speak like this, we are suggesting that within matter itself are the forms and potentials of divine expression and existence. To consider the world of matter and the world of Spirit as equally acceptable vehicles for the divine presence, to suggest that matter is not a second-rate expression of holiness and God, makes many of us uncomfortable — even though we have moved away from the idea of matter as corrupt, a sign of our "fallen" nature, and have come to recognize matter as at least neutral. But what if we said that matter is intrinsically good, that although matter can be temporarily distorted or adapted, its own unique goodness will ultimately prevail? So whatever is becoming will realize the good it ought to be, regardless of any side-paths or alternate routes it takes, or is forced to take, in its becoming. And whatever is becoming can recognize the good in itself from the beginning to the ending of its journey. It will not be identical to its origins, because it can "remember" the journey; but it will be the fuller version of itself, the harvesting of wisdom, experience, and promise.

THE GARDEN OF EDEN: A STORY OF BECOMING

One way to think about sacred history is as the record of a people being refashioned and choosing ways to be and to become. The most encouraging thing about the stories of the Hebrew people is their immediacy and reality. In these tales, poems, and legends, there are few people who are totally evil, and no people without tragic flaws. They are like us; and so we can identify with their struggles, losses, and triumphs. These narratives mark an evolution of consciousness that could be called "humanity growing up." Other cultures share similar histories, although the interpretation of the stories may vary.[5]

For our purposes here, we are going to reflect on the very first story in the Hebrew/Christian Bible, the story of beginnings — but what beginnings? We hear that, when the earth is formed, it is GOOD. When people are formed, they are GOOD. Then a new narrator enters the story.

> In the day that God made the earth and the heavens, when no plant of the field was yet in the earth and no herb of the field had yet sprung up ... God formed adamah[6] from the dust of the ground, and breathed into his nostrils the breath of life; and the man became a living being. And God planted a garden in Eden, in the east; and there he put the man whom he had formed. Out of the ground God made to grow every tree that is pleasant to the sight and good for food, the tree of life also in the midst of the garden, and the tree of the knowledge of good and evil....
>
> God took the man and put him in the garden of Eden to till it and keep it. And God commanded the man, "You may freely eat of every tree of the garden; but of the tree of the knowledge of good and evil you shall not eat, for in the day that you eat of it you shall die."
>
> Then God said, "It is not good that the man should be alone; I will make him a helper as his partner." ... And the rib that God had taken from the man he made into a woman and brought her to the man.... And the man and his wife were both naked, and were not ashamed.

Up to this point, the humans resemble the rest of the animals in their simplicity, but then a new element is introduced into the story.

Now the serpent was more crafty than any other wild animal that God had made. He said to the woman, "Did God say, 'You shall not eat from any tree in the garden'?" The woman said to the serpent, "We may eat of the fruit of the trees in the garden; but God said, 'You shall not eat of the fruit of the tree that is in the middle of the garden, nor shall you touch it, or you shall die.' " But the serpent said to the woman, "You will not die; for God knows that when you eat of it your eyes will be opened, and you will be like God, knowing good and evil." So when the woman saw that the tree was good for food, and that it was a delight to the eyes, and that the tree was to be desired to make one wise, she took of its fruit and ate; and she also gave some to her husband, who was with her, and he ate. Then the eyes of both were opened, and they knew that they were naked; and they sewed fig leaves together and made loincloths for themselves.

They heard the sound of God walking in the garden at the time of the evening breeze, and the man and his wife hid themselves from the presence of God among the trees of the garden. But God called to the man, and said to him, "Where are you?" He said, "I heard the sound of you in the garden, and I was afraid, because I was naked; and I hid myself." He said, "Who told you that you were naked? Have you eaten from the tree of which I commanded you not to eat?" The man said, "The woman whom you gave to be with me, she gave me fruit from the tree, and I ate." Then God said to the woman, "What is this that you have done?" The woman said, "The serpent tricked me, and I ate." …

The man named his wife Eve, because she was the mother of all living. And God made garments of skins for the man and for his wife, and clothed them.

Then God said, "See, the man has become like one of us, knowing good and evil; and now, he might reach out his hand and take also from the tree of life, and eat, and live forever" — therefore the God sent him forth from the garden of Eden, to till the ground from which he was taken. He drove out the man; and at the east of the garden of Eden he placed the cherubim, and a sword flaming and turning to guard the way to the tree of life.

[Genesis 2:4–3:24]

This narrator is concerned about why, if God is good and creation is good, there is so much suffering in the world, why humanity created in the image of God feels estranged from the holiness of God. The answer for millennia has been that humanity "fell" from grace, because we disobeyed a fairly simple directive. The story is, of course, layered and shadowed with many possibilities.

In certain extra-canonical interpretations, such as those favoured by the early Gnostic and Manichean sects, humanity is implicated in a cosmic battle between the moral forces of good and evil. Genesis tells, accordingly, the story of the first battle. The Dead Sea Scrolls speak of a future battle. "On the day the Kittians fall, there shall be mighty combat and carnage in the presence of the God of Israel, for this is the day he appointed of old for the final battle against the Sons of Darkness."[7]

By another way of thinking, humanity is offered choices and opportunities for self-definition. According to this understanding, God becomes the guide rather than the ruler of cosmic destiny. The Holy One allows creation to open and develop with nudges — some more forceful than others — but the principle of randomness and freedom informs both divine and human reality. I think that, regardless of the original intentions of the author(s) of Genesis, this interpretation offers us room to explore how an intrinsically good creation might develop into a dynamic universe that, if planned at all, is sketched only in rough outline.

But then why the "fall" and where the evil? If we allow the principle of randomness and freedom to be characteristics of goodness and holiness, then we can read the story of Genesis with the metaphorical assumption that nothing but God's creation inhabited the garden. The serpent in the garden carries all the ambivalence of that ancient symbol of testing and healing, of challenges and beginnings. To consider other instances where serpents have power, we could remember the serpent Moses holds up in the wilderness.

> Then God sent poisonous serpents among the people, and they bit the people, so that many Israelites died. The people came to Moses and said, "We have sinned by speaking against God and against you; pray to God to take away the serpents from us." So Moses prayed for the people. And God said to Moses, "Make a poisonous serpent, and

set it on a pole; and everyone who is bitten shall look at it and live." So Moses made a serpent of bronze, and put it upon a pole; and whenever a serpent bit someone, that person would look at the serpent of bronze and live.
[Numbers 21:6–9]

In the ancient world serpents represented wisdom, healing, and eternal life as well as death. We see one symbolic remnant from Greece in the caduceus, the staff of Hermes or Mercury, the symbol on contemporary doctors' diplomas. It was a common belief that the snake was virtually immortal and lived a new life after it had shed its skin.[8] The seraphim were represented as fiery serpents — messengers and reflectors of the divine fire.[9] The serpent carried a weight of intention and meaning; it was not simply a seducer, but rather one who tests — God's prosecutor and healer,[10] a principle of possibility and uncertainty in the midst, and as part of, goodness.

In the Christian era, we can look at the gospel story in which Jesus is compared not to Moses but to the serpent. "And just as Moses lifted up the serpent in the wilderness, so must the Son of Man be lifted up, that whoever believes in him may have eternal life" [John 3:14]. Jesus carries the incarnation of the Creator (intrinsic goodness) and the mission of the serpent to test and heal. Gnostics would recognize this line of imagery, but they would often see it as condemnation of the God who set limits on human freedom. "[One radical Gnostic] teacher dared to tell the story of Paradise from the serpent's point of view, and depicted the serpent as a teacher of divine wisdom who desperately tried to get

Adam and Eve to open their eyes to their creator's true and despicable nature."[11] I am suggesting that the serpent of the Genesis story may be viewed as one of the metaphorical agents of the Divine, who wills growth and development for creation, not as an adversary but as a teacher. In my view the Creator is not despicable; rather the Creator is the one who empowers transformation, who encourages goodness and growth.

In the Genesis story, the serpent invites the people to open their eyes, to share in the self-knowledge and awareness that could be their inheritance as creatures of the Holy One. And so they bite and their eyes are opened — the "fortunate fall."[12] They become like God, knowing good and evil, knowing suffering and shame, the pain of birth and fear of death. Traditionally this story is seen as the curse of humanity; however, the punishment (or the reward) is not death but awareness. Death is just the normal course of embodiment. Awareness, enlightenment, is the normal course of spirit. The first people suddenly recognize themselves as separate, different; and they are afraid. And so they cover themselves with leaves as if they were still part of the environment, as if they were not separate, although they always were. But now they know.

The "curse" that people bring upon themselves is to evolve into being more than domestic animals, to trade in a sense of blissful ignorance for awareness and individuality. With this evolution comes a share in the responsibilities of being like a god, having power over the environment we inhabit, the animals we dominate, the other people with whom we share the earth, the way we interpret the purpose of our existence, our capacity for awe and wonder and love and cruelty. And who suffers the most for this choice? We assume that people do, but they experience only what aware-ness causes them to interpret as pain and labour. The one who invites us to grow up (the serpent), and the earth upon which we walk, receive the full burden of our choice.

> cursed are you among all animals
> and among all wild creatures;
> upon your belly you shall go,
> and dust you shall eat
> all the days of your life ...
> And to the man he said, ...
> cursed is the ground because of you.
> [Genesis 3:14–17]

The second creation story tells of humanity becoming con-scious, self-activating, autonomous to some extent. It is the story of the day we left home because we wanted to make our own the rules. The question is not whether we can get back into the garden, but whether we will accept account-ability for being like the gods, the responsibility of living interdependently with our environment, the possibility of understanding suffering not as punishment but as the real-ity of being self-aware and self-activating. We have our own gardens now, and we are invited to use them with the aware-ness and knowledge with which we have been endowed.

In 1 Corinthians, Paul compared Jesus and *adamah*, the first human:

Thus it is written, "The first man, Adam, became a living being"; the last Adam became a life-giving spirit. But it is not the spiritual that is first, but the physical, and then the spiritual. The first man was from the earth, a man of dust; the second man is from heaven. As was the man of dust, so are those who are of the dust; and as is the man of heaven, so are those who are of heaven. Just as we have borne the image of the man of dust, we will also bear the image of the man of heaven.

[1 Corinthians 15:45–49]

In Romans 5, Paul thought about the first man, *adamah*, as the "type"[13] of the one who was to come; that is, *adamah* enfleshes the creativity of God and begins the cycle of consciousness. But it is the Christ who calls us to recognize the Divine in the human, the possibility of Life within the constraints of creation, of flesh.

Perhaps another way of considering *adamah* and Jesus might be to say that, in them, we see that even in the time of trial, there is goodness and new life, that our very limitations as humans can provide us with new ways to live, new insights into how we do, and do not, participate in the Divine. The first human experienced the terror of separation, the fear of abandonment by the parent, the thrill of a new beginning, the need to form community and make a new home. But the Holy One cared for these first people; they were given clothes and they remained in relationship. Nor did they die immediately; in fact, they multiplied. Jesus walks into human life and faces the terror of abandonment, the risk of wisdom, the pain of loving; through his apparent separation from the Divine, a new vision is born.

MATTER

In one way, the first creation story in Genesis is about the birth of goodness into matter. And matter is not neutral; nor is it corrupt. It is divine, made from the divine substance. The Holy One nurtures it, as a bird cares for its young, brooding over creation, or as air inspires a newborn body, causing it to quicken.

> In the beginning when God created the heavens and the earth, the earth was a formless void and darkness covered the face of the deep, while a wind from God swept over the face of the waters.
>
> [Genesis 1:1–2]

The text says that God made something from nothing. If the only thing existing was the Creator, then the Creator used the Divine-self to create. The creation is imprinted with holiness in the beginning; right from the start, the Creator hums and pats and caresses the creation with approval and delight.

THE SABBATH RHYTHM

When the Creator regards the world, the Creator is seeing the Divine-self in its potential and its completion. When we consider the quality that we describe as goodness, we understand it not merely as a state of being but as a kinetic verb, a movement of holiness. First the Creator works, and then the Creator appreciates — two activities that tell us about the action of goodness in our lives. If everything is good, then the Creator's actions are likewise good. Therefore, we can say that both work and Sabbath (rest or appreciation) are blessed expressions of God's goodness.

Creation, in its cosmic dance, steps through eternity with a Sabbath rhythm — first the work, then the rest, then the work.[14] The void, the matter, the void. The potential, the actual, the potential. Matter is good, potential is good. The work is good, and the resting is good. Neutrinos race away from the sun, then collapse into the explosion of a new creation. In one moment we "make," and in the next moment we appreciate that which we have made. We are and we are not; then we are. The implications of this are far-reaching in terms of how we regard our lives and the reason for our existence.

If we never pause, though, we will never regard what we are making in either an evaluative or appreciative way. And if we are afraid to stop, then what are we saying about how we are using the gift of life that we have received? To stop and appreciate the work is at least as important as the work itself, because reflecting on what we have accomplished enables us to see the value, the "goodness," of what we have done. It is in the Sabbath moments that we recognize our link to holiness and the inestimable value of each life, each artefact of the Maker of all. It is in the resting that we ask ourselves if we are working in harmony and collaboration with holiness, or if we are making a pointless distortion that hides, rather than reveals, holiness.

We need to ask ourselves what our intentional work is. Is it what gives us income, or is it what matters deeply to us? We may work on a construction crew, building roads. We might receive from those roads a satisfaction that we have built well, or we might regard those roads as not our lifework at all. Our lifework may be in parenting or ecological concerns, or in using a talent such as music to gladden others. We are the ones who choose our purpose in the world, and we are the evaluators and appreciators of our labour.

Nonetheless, to indict and isolate oneself by forgetting Sabbath (understood as the fallow time, the time for appreciation) is the tragedy of those whose work offers no meaning and no connection to the original act of God's will. Such work is lifeless and lacking the breath of holiness, the *ruah* of God, the wind sweeping over the waters. To continue such activity is to bankrupt the soul of its original goodness and energy; to distance oneself from the Source of life. It is the death of spirit in this life.

Unfortunately, such work is rarely the choice of individuals. We are caught in systems that need to be rethought and reconfigured within the parameters of a life-oriented plan, in which the well-being of all individuals is the highest priority. While work that is not life-oriented does destroy people and societies in time, I am not convinced that it has any ultimate ontological effect, or changes the true nature of reality. To make sense of what has happened to us, we may want to reflect on our use of life, and our appreciation or abuse of the created order, for ourselves and our children. To be hopeful is to have long vision. Sadly, we will not realize the peaceable kingdom within our lifetime. For most of the world, life is about struggle and suffering and early death.

It is difficult to believe that, in the immediate future, goodness could develop from the perversity of much human behaviour. It is far more tempting to relinquish hope, in exchange for a weary cynicism. To perceive and trust in goodness requires either great spirit or the discipline to find an oasis of peace and freedom, to intentionally base our lives on the premise of abundance for all. The work of the third millennium is to create a new set of conditions, values, and expectations for human life and the world. Each society and culture will need to work through the lenses of their own belief systems.

Evil

Goodness is the essence of life. Evil is a turning from goodness. The opposite of evil, therefore, is not goodness itself but, more appropriately, the *search* for goodness. We name something evil when it tends to bend the signs of goodness, or to put obstacles in the path of developing goodness. I believe that evil is a moral quality and is socially determined. I do not believe in a horned man or an angel who presides over Hell. It is helpful to remind ourselves that the Gehenna of the gospels was a city dump for the earthly Jerusalem, not for the heavenly city. Perhaps Jesus was not suggesting eternal damnation so much as calling some people "trash," a distasteful idea but not an eternal dictum. We must not let ourselves be lazy in how we hear these stories. They are calls to action, to "wake up" and participate in our lives and in the unfolding life of the world.

Premises of faith and acts of intellectual and spiritual discipline help us to impose meaning on the world as we experience it. The way we impose order and organization on the world has something to do with how we understand the point of being alive. In a linear world, we think of order as moving from one stage to another, moving from conception to birth to death, or from idea to design to prototype to completion to obsolescence. This is a fairly tidy process, and it allows humans a sense of control that excludes randomness, except as accidental. Assembly-line thinking comforts us more than anything. In this model, obedience and following directions are the best way; the opportunity to daydream, to reflect, to step outside the boundaries, is dangerous and impractical. It is why we hold artists in an ambivalence of suspicion and admiration. They dare to colour outside the lines, to express our deepest fears and longings without regard for socio-cultural norms.

In an apparently static system, we can easily assign meaning and purpose to whatever happens, because order suggests predictability, not surprise. It also allows us to relegate what does not fit the system into a tidy category that we name evil. By this understanding, evil is anything that will not fit the conveyor belt; evil is that which seems "other" to us, or "abnormal." We think of cancer as abnormal and evil, when in fact it is simply a natural product whose primary offence is to threaten our lives. Indeed, anything that threatens what we perceive to be the natural order — on the assembly line — is deemed to be evil. Further, I want to ask: Is something that harms us necessarily evil? Is something that threatens us evil? Is an earthquake evil? A supernova? The Ebola virus? Is unhappiness or suffering the result of evil, or simply of being alive?

Evil can be assigned to any breach of conformity, whether that breach causes surprise or harm, brings a fresh breath of creativity or a new genetic development. But I would say that this is not an adequate definition of evil. Instead, true evil actually requires conformity in a way that is foreign to goodness. And conformity is not the only ingredient; but fatigue, despair, overwork, and oppression can contribute to the way we view the world and ourselves. Evil is the distortion of how we understand our own beauty and essential divinity. Evil is the result of doubting that we and everyone else are made for joy and goodness. Evil is the by-product of disrespect for the holiness around and within us, and it can destroy everyone and everything it touches. Whenever an appreciation and reverence for an individual life is suspended for the sake of a belief, an idea, a political agenda, or a program of conformity, the seeds of evil have been sown.

Elie Weisel once said, " We have seen the metamorphosis of history, and now it is our duty to bear witness. When one people is destined to die, all others are implicated. When one ethnic group is humiliated, humanity is threatened. Hitler's plans to annihilate the Jewish people and to decimate the Slavic nations bore the germ of universal death. Jews were killed, but humankind was assassinated."[15] Evil requires uniforms, that is, conformity, for the oppressor and uniforms, or nakedness, for the abused. Both oppressor and victim become categories, no longer real lives, no longer human either in pity or in conscience. Evil dehumanizes everyone into roles and functions; as Weisel said at the Barbie trial, "Declared to be less than a man, and therefore deserving neither compassion nor pity, the Jew was born only to die — just as the killer was born only to kill.... Except for Hoss ... no killer has repented. Their logic? There had to be executioners to eliminate a million and a half Jewish children; killers were needed to annihilate four and a half million Jewish adults."[16]

In the early church, evil was thought to be a prowling predator or an inevitable flaw in "fallen" human nature. Evil was either a demonic outer force or an ineluctable inner malady, "original sin." We have a great deal of difficulty in accepting responsibility for evil. But evil is always an individual or collective choice, developed in the context of a society. I am suggesting that evil is a distortion in how we view life and the world, each other and God. Evil has great power because it has the same beginnings as goodness, but evil is like trying to see oneself in moving water or in a broken mirror. For me, it is like trying to thread a needle without bifocals — impossible and frustrating.

Evil attempts to narrow the choices, limit freedom, discourage intuition. The search for goodness requires that we think new thoughts, open ourselves to change, welcome diversity and growth, see the world from every perspective we can imagine. The search for goodness looks for the Divine in others and, therefore, avoids intentional harm. Evil rules that maintaining order and doctrine may require harsh methods for the sake of a present, or supposed future, social benefit.

The cold comfort about the artefacts of evil is that, while devastating in the present and nearer future, they are nonetheless doomed to dissolution. What is redeemed after great suffering is goodness, holiness, the clear vision that always returns to us, as the compass returns to its northerly point. So true evil is ultimately futile, but it has devastating power in the present to obscure the self-awareness of our innate holiness, our equilibrium, to make us doubt our true nature as children of the Divine. I want to resist the constriction of vision and purpose that is evil, because I want to see more goodness in my life. I want to experience more of the deep satisfaction, the sense of abundance, that is God's seventh-day delight. And most of all, I want to know that I live in a society focused on the search for goodness, rather than mechanisms of control.

AUTHENTIC GOODNESS

Socially, we have created a caricature of goodness. It has come to mean following the rules, avoiding change, behaving in "natural ways," obeying the script, being nice. But what if none of this has anything to do with goodness at all? What if authentic goodness is about becoming, evolving, changing; breaking things and making them new; breaking ourselves and healing others so that we can be new; dying so that we may live, and suffering so that we may grow? What if randomness is part of the nature of the Divine, and what if we are most like the Creator when we allow for the Heisenberg principle of uncertainty in our lives?[17] What if resigning ourselves to participation in assembly-line thinking is indeed evil? What if reversing our notions of social good, redefining sensible thinking, would free us from many of our collective failures? The teaching of Jesus was so radically opposed to "sensible" thinking that the gospel writers recorded some of his sayings, possibly in their own surprise and confusion about what he could have meant by them.

> For the kingdom of heaven is like a landowner who went out early in the morning to hire labourers for his vineyard. After agreeing with the labourers for the usual daily wage, he sent them into his vineyard. When he went out about nine o'clock, he saw others standing idle in the marketplace; and he said to them, "You also go into the vineyard, and I will pay you whatever is right." So they went. When he went out again about noon and about three o'clock, he did the same. And about five o'clock he went out and found others standing around; and he said to them, "Why are you standing here idle all day?" They said to him, "Because no one has hired us." He said to them, "You also go into the vineyard." When evening came, the owner of the vineyard said to his manager, "Call the labourers and give them their pay, beginning with the last and then going to the first." When those hired about five o'clock came, each of them received the usual daily wage. Now when the first came, they thought they would receive more; but each of them also received the usual daily wage.
> [Matthew 20:1–10]

Or:

> "Whoever wants to be first must be last of all and servant of all." Then he took a little child and put it among them; and taking it in his arms, he said to them, "Whoever welcomes one such child in my name welcomes me, and whoever welcomes me welcomes not me but the one who sent me."
>
> [Mark 9:35–37]

These are examples of a way of life that values humans as living beings rather than as commodities to be bought, sold, and manipulated for short-term satisfaction. Goodness is revealed in the clarity and simplicity of these responses. Allow people what they need rather than what they deserve; practise humility and cherish it in others. To see the world in this manner is to stand with the Creator at the beginning and the end, to know that all things made are "very good," and to love creation with a fierce and protective passion. It is the true eschatological position to see in both the newborn and the dying, in both the neutrino and the universe, the hands of the divine artisan. It is to stand with Christ at the cross for love and loss, in hope and solidarity. It is to say that this creation is good enough to die for, that humanity is loved enough to die with. To share this perspective opens the possibility of ourselves as creators also, ourselves as those who make what is good. It is to remind ourselves that all matter is good, and is being transformed by God and by us.

I like to think about creation as clay, as paint, as Word

developing form, only to elude definition just as it solidifies. If this is so, then evolution is not matter in decay but chaos becoming order we recognize, becoming chaos we fear, becoming order we do not recognize. I like to think of chaos as unconstructed matter, awaiting the intervention of form. Then form must be thought of as transitional, awaiting recreation:

> This teacher tells us we must ride the unknown. She has made many pots. She says we cannot rely on a formula. She has made pot after pot over many years and she says she still rides the unknown…. She says every rule we have memorized … every law must yield to experience. She says we must learn from each act, and no act is ever the same…. The possibilities, we see, never end. And when we take the vessel out of the fire, our teacher tells us, we will always be surprised.
>
> "The Possible," Susan Griffin[18]

This becomes a truth both in the microcosm of the person and in the macrocosm of the universe. Our lives move through different phases, from ovum and zygote to maturity and finally death, but in between there are many stages. Either we are reinvented by external change in our lives, or we choose to recreate ourselves to satisfy a yearning for transformation. Nothing in the universe appears to be fixed except this originating principle of goodness, the expression of which is open-ended and into which we have been invited.

If the ethical standard for Christians is indeed the search for goodness, and evil is a detour on the path, then what shall we do about the concept of sin? Every time of turning from awareness of self, of others, to an illusion of our "nest" time when we could hide from our true natures, becomes an opportunity for sin. In reality, such times are blended moment by moment as we choose and reject different ways of being alive, different self-definitions. It is a bit like an old union song, "Whose side are you on?" And it ought to haunt us when we forget that, in every decision, we are making this choice. Such choice is usually complex, and only hindsight will assure us of our wisdom in the choosing. We all know times in personal relationships when we wish we could change the events, and would if it were only possible. We all remember things we have said that now we would swallow or disavow. And we all have the experience of something turning out much better than we had hoped. There are no guarantees in the choosing.

The Gnostics thought that we could escape our human limitations by special knowledge and introduction to a particular construction of mystery, but in fact it is the ordinariness of life that holds the secret. It is in solidarity with all of the creation that we discover the truth of our human nature. Part of this truth lies in humility as we acknowledge that we are still in process, that to move along further we must change and grow in tolerance and compassion. We need training to learn how to select for goodness. The new doctrines need to help us cooperate with the goodness within, to resist being intellectually and spiritually boxed in. We all know that we will have to bring an end to war and find ways to live carefully with our environment. But we are reluctant to accept that such social change requires a mass conversion of the heart. The task of Christians is to cultivate ourselves so that we may be yeast in the dough, working invisibly but effectively to turn disparate elements into what nourishes and satisfies hunger. This task is about becoming mature, full of grace and humility, accepting our limits and laughing at our tendency to see ourselves as all of God rather than brilliant stained-glass shards of the Creator.

To return to the metaphor of the garden: Is growing up good? Well, it depends on the history into which we have been born, and the ways in which we learn to grapple with our place in the world. For each person and society, a level of reflection is required to decide how we will change and what we will change. In our time, we are encouraged to see decision making as too complex for the average human. Although we complain, we are happy to let the powers and principalities have the driver's seat. I hope this makes everyone profoundly uncomfortable! Anyone who has read Aldous Huxley has had adequate warning about the horror of relinquishing responsibility to faceless power. When asked about a coin, Jesus replied somewhat archly that one should give Caesar his own. But what belongs to Caesar anyway? Is the world understood to be a divine creation? Whose plan has ascendancy, whose reality needs to be lifted up, which pragmatism offers life and growth, and which offers death?[19] Once we are able to recognize the boundary between Caesar and holiness, then we will begin the next stage of human development.

THE QUESTIONS FROM THE GARDEN

The questions from the garden are not frivolous questions. They are not about gender or obedience, but they are about power and responsibility. They are about accepting a choice, a destiny that is unplanned, that is created as we go along the path of history. If Jesus is the incarnation of God, then this incarnation resides partially in each one of us, to be used for good or ill, for healing or punishment. Most particularly, this incarnation is of concern to Christians as it resides in the church. What people identify with when they hear about Jesus are the organizations of the church; so we had better consider carefully what picture of Jesus we are offering the world.

Christians are required not only to do no harm but to fix what we have broken, to account for what we have let slip, to grow where we have ravaged, and to be transparent in our actions. I think we have learned that frightening the faithful with eternal damnation, or the devil, has a limited efficacy. The twin spectres of poverty and violence stalk our world. Jesus in the gospel of Matthew charges his disciples with a mission of feeding the hungry, clothing the naked, providing comfort and sanctuary. This is, after all, what he did. We say casually in the church that Jesus died that we might live; so what does this say about our lives? What is the task of discipleship? Pick up your cross, give a drink to these little ones, bless those who curse you, leave your gift at the altar and go to your enemy, and so on. It is not ambiguous, just demanding!

Heraclitus said that you can never step into the same river twice, and this is obviously true, as anyone knows who has ever attempted to return to the nest, to go home. To understand that the water is changing, the flow is changing, we are changing, that the whole of creation is imbued with the radiance of the divine, is to decide that we are either polluters and pillagers, or pilgrims and healers. The water will ultimately spiral to its true nature — with or despite us. But how and who will we be in the water? I think that we have followed Jesus, at least partly, because we want to hear, "This day you are my Beloved. I am well pleased in you."

In all things, goodness.

Source of our beginning and refuge of our ending,
open up to us the pathway of discovery.
Grant us eyes to see your goodness reflected in the whole of creation.
Open our hearts to love your world and to journey with you in confidence
and in the sure and certain hope that we are yours forever.
We ask this in the power of love that is the risen Christ.
Amen.

In Change,
Wisdom

learning to hear the question that
teaches me to hear the question …

In the last chapter, I said that one of the attributes of goodness is diversity and growth. This is in sharp contrast to our inherited ideas about the unchanging nature of the Divine, about fixed truths that can be understood by us, about stability as a desirable quality. When we say that we are born out of goodness and are journeying through goodness, we have changed our assumptions about the meaning of life and the nature of the Divine. We are no longer fallen creatures, working out our deliverance through an unknowable plan, but participants in, and artists of, the universe.

The biblical record assures us of God's steadfast love, but the Bible also speaks of a God who has changes of heart and intention. We too change in how we understand our relationship to God, and this also is recorded in our Bible. Although it makes us anxious, the reality is that everything is in the process of transformation. To accept the twin principles of learning (wisdom) and change affects not only our formulation of doctrine, but our understanding of mission and membership. In a world of discovery, no idea remains untested, no ethic ceases to require re-evaluation.

From a conviction that humanity stood at the centre of creation, we are learning to see ourselves as tiny flashes of consciousness in an incomprehensibly vast cosmos. Instead of language and metaphor that underline the immutability of God and the universe, we need to rethink our doctrines and rehear the stories in a way that emphasizes the concept of change and adaptation in the Divine, and that accepts learning as a spiritual discipline for humanity. Instead of stability and a fixed plan, we need to develop a doctrine of randomness and opportunity.

THE WISDOM TRADITION

The Wisdom literature arose in an era not unlike ours,[20] an era of secularism, of cynicism about institutional religion, a time of questioning about relating to God. In this chapter we will examine how the Wisdom tradition can provide a basis for our thinking. The contemporary search for Wisdom is a holy search, a way for us to come to terms with living in a world that we now know will always be changing, in a universe that is being transformed.

The most common word for wisdom in Hebrew scriptures is *chokmah*, with its root sense of both learning and teaching understanding. Although there are several other words that suggest intelligence or craftiness, *chokmah* is by far the most common.[21] It is an attribute or expression of the Divine, but it is also a quest for humanity. To say one is searching for the Divine is to say one is seeking Wisdom. While Wisdom to some extent defines the Creator, or speaks of a quality of the Creator, it is also part of the "becoming" of humanity; it is never realized but is always a stage of our development.

One version of the search for Wisdom by humans is found in the creation story in Genesis, as we read in the previous chapter. In Proverbs 8:22–35, there is another creation story that sets Holy Wisdom at the beginning of the beginning.

God created me at the beginning of his work,
the first of his acts of long ago.
Ages ago I was set up, at the first, before the beginning of
the earth.

When there were no depths I was brought forth,
when there were no springs abounding with water.
Before the mountains had been shaped, before the hills, I
was brought forth....
When he marked out the foundations of the earth,
then I was beside him, like a master worker; and I was
daily his delight,
rejoicing before him always, rejoicing in his inhabited
world
and delighting in the human race.
And now, my children, listen to me: happy are those who
keep my ways.
Hear instruction and be wise, and do not neglect it.
Happy is the one who listens to me....
For whoever finds me finds life
and obtains favour from the Holy One;
but those who miss me injure themselves;
all who hate me love death.

Wisdom as a personification of God found a strong place in its own form of literature. This literature considered how to live a life that was both spiritual and worldly — that is, a life that was centred on the Divine but respected the life of the body as well. Although some of the wisdom literature encouraged the study of Torah, it showed scant concern for cultic or institutional matters.[22] It was more concerned with the development of humans and our social selves. Its interest lay in living a life that would promote *shalom* and well-being for all. We read in it a remarkable lack of interest in how to worship, and a striking focus on how to understand life as we experience it. The Divine functions as a more or less unknowable Creator who is revealed through Holy Wisdom in the Torah and in the prophets.

For some of these later writers Wisdom was a goal in herself; while for others she was, like the prophets, another expression of Torah and God's will. In the literature, Wisdom calls people to amend their lives, to examine their souls more deeply, to seek her above all else in this life. It is a call to learning — not a well-developed concept in Christianity. As R. B. Y. Scott said, "Inherent in the idea of wisdom [is] that it could be taught, whether as a technical craft, as rules for the good life, or as a profound understanding of the meaning of human existence."[23]

LEARNING

To learn anything means to be changed, but often Christianity has substituted adherence to dogma for true learning. Commenting on Tertullian, Elaine Pagels notes that, in their efforts to contain the Gnostic movement, the fathers of the church branded even questioning as leading to heresy, and set the stage for 2,000 years of dogmatic and unthinking obedience.[24] The doctrinal "enemy" became not the Gnostics so much as inquiry or independent theological reflection. This fear of original or creative thinking extends into our own time, as we worry about which is the correct liturgical form, what may or may not be said in pulpit or book, who is a member and who an outsider. It sets doctrine in opposition to revelation and inspiration.

Learning is always about the surprise of revelation and about mindfulness — attention to the experiences we and others have, including the experiences we have come to call tradition. What we are learning bit by bit, and in a conditional way, reveals the reality that is observed by God. I say "conditional" because it seems to me that we never will be filled with the whole understanding of anything; our understanding will always be partial, unless we too are transformed. Matthew warns that our expectations and assumptions will trick and blind us to what is reality: "For John came neither eating nor drinking, and they say, 'He has a demon'; the Son of Man came eating and drinking, and they say, 'Look, a glutton and a drunkard, a friend of tax collectors and sinners!' Yet wisdom is vindicated by her deeds" [Matthew 11:18–19]. Since we come out to see the prophet and the God that is already inside us, our preparation to encounter the Divine affects our picture of this Holiness. Were John and Jesus charlatans, possessed by egomania, or were they possessed by spirits of passion and insight?

Learning helps us to see clearly, to wipe some of the fog off the metaphorical mirror of St. Paul: "For now we see in a mirror, dimly, but then we will see face to face. Now I know only in part; then I will know fully, even as I have been fully known" [1 Corinthians 13:12]. Revelation of reality, seeing the world with the clarity of the Holy One, would fulfill what Paul yearned to experience in the resurrection. It is the hope of seeing without the veil, of fulfilling Moses' dream — to see the Holy and live [Exodus 33:18–21]. At any moment, we can only approach the knowledge and understanding of God. Our awareness of the cosmos paints a vastly bigger picture than it did in the days of either Moses or St. Paul. Despite our increased knowledge, our more sophisticated technology, we know that continued learning will expand our present expectations and assumptions. Yet we still want to "see" God, just as people came to "see" Jesus, to experience the hope and wonder that cannot be meaningfully named.

TRUTH

The wisdom literature suggests that God's Holy Wisdom is always active in the world, inviting the seeker to learn more, to understand deeper, to turn from the ephemeral to the eternal, even if this search makes the institutions of religion uncomfortable. Wisdom acquires, tests, and refines knowledge, until it becomes our understanding of divine reality. We probably could not say finally what piece of knowledge has become truth for us, although many preachers insist that they have God and truth wrapped up and pinned down. But we can speak about what we yearn to be true, what the Divine is for us right now. The debate about whether the nature of God is unfolding is purely speculative. We cannot know anything about the Divine beyond what we have understood through our own experience, through the metaphors and stories we create to explain the presence of the Divine in our midst, and through revelation as we have understood it to this point. There are many questions about our perceptions and the conditions that affect them, but we can say that this particular time and place frames what we understand and hope right now.

Consider an example of learning and shifting conscious-ness. During the time of "flat earth" cosmology, the idea of Jesus physically ascending to join Elijah and God in heaven was concrete and plausible, or at least a workable metaphor. In our literalistic and scientific age, this metaphor of ascen-sion no longer works. Instead, we have to speak of different dimensions of reality, of breaks in the space–time continuum, of matter that has a fluid nature like light or oxygen, and of things that travel so fast they can be in two places at the same time. This would have sounded like speculative fiction in 1960, but now we have new scientific awareness, new knowl-edge, to bring to the metaphor. To teach children about the ascension story today means an emphasis not on Jesus "go-ing up" to sit on a heavenly throne, but on a transformed Christ coming around and into our hearts and lives. To teach the ascension is part of the acceptance that nothing ever re-mains the same, that what we love may be so transformed that it ceases to be recognizable in its previously known form.

Wisdom means to learn, to acquire knowledge, to change what we understand as truth. This may be a threatening in-sight, but it is merely the beginning for the seeker of Wisdom — to understand that nothing a person presently believes is necessarily fixed in its present form.

Most of us have had the experience of wanting to deny a piece of knowledge because it so deeply conflicts with what we have trusted to be truth. To cross this boundary is to en-ter into a holy space, a wilderness, recognizable by feelings of fear, awe, and liberation. The experience of the burning bush is one of Moses' many moments of stepping into the wilderness of new ideas. In this story, God "waits" to see if

Moses is ready and willing to notice something so anomalous in nature that it must speak of the Divine. When Moses turns to examine this strange sight, God responds with revelation. Moses' life will be forever changed by this experience. His self-understanding, the nature of his lifestyle and community — everything about him will be overthrown by the power of what he learns and comes to understand.

> Moses ... came to Horeb, the mountain of God. There the angel of the Holy One appeared to him in a flame of fire out of a bush; he looked, and the bush was blazing, yet it was not consumed. Then Moses said, "I must turn aside and look at this great sight, and see why the bush is not burned up." ... [God said] "The place on which you are standing is holy ground."
>
> [Exodus 3:1–5]

THE FREEDOM OF GOD

Learning requires openness, vulnerability to risk, and a willingness to realize something we have not known before. Our partner in this endeavour is our Creator who waits for us, encourages us, tests us, and allows us to decide. Such generosity of spirit suggests that God is able to live with more than one version of the story as it unfolds. The "plan" is just that — a series of possibilities, some seen, some that will surprise us. We have tried desperately to impose an immutability on the Divine, despite numerous biblical references to God's independence and changeability — God's own repentance.

Because we are mortal and so little is fixed for us, we would prefer to have someone, something, in a fixed order, even if we hate its judgements. The story of Jonah is a case in point. God decides that the repentance of the people of Nineveh is acceptable and spares them [Jonah 3:10]. But Jonah, the prophet of doom, is displeased that the Holy One has had a change of heart, and he responds in a petulant tantrum, objecting to God's mercy and forgiveness [Jonah 4:1–5].

Jonah steadfastly hopes that God will visit disaster upon the people — unlike Abraham who attempts to save the righteous people of Sodom, dealing and bargaining with God for divine clemency and forbearance.

> Then Abraham came near and said, "Will you indeed sweep away the righteous with the wicked? Suppose there are fifty righteous within the city; will you then sweep away the place and not forgive it for the fifty righteous who are in it? Far be it from you to do such a thing, to slay the righteous with the wicked, so that the righteous fare as the wicked! Far be that from you! Shall not the Judge of all the earth do what is just?" ... Then he said, "Oh do not let the Lord be angry if I speak just once more. Suppose ten are found there." He answered, "For the sake of ten I will not destroy it."
>
> [Genesis 18:23–33]

These stories teach us about the freedom of God to show that we are either participants in mercy or prisoners of our own egos and vengeful spirits. To be a partner with God is to accept freedom and changeability, indeed to encourage change for the growth of goodness and mercy.

We read in Judeo-Christian scripture that change is the only constant in the universe, that we are called to change, called to develop wisdom, called to become like God, to become mature, complete. We are called to grow, to become "perfect" — from the Greek word *teleios*, which means fully grown, fully realized [Matthew 5:48]. This suggests that being made in the divine image means to be becoming, to be works in progress. And it may mean that the Holy One is changing too, or that God is the paradox of being, already complete but unfolding in the divine revelation to humanity.

Spirit and Flesh

One thing we know is that everything in creation appears to have the potential for change; at root everything is becoming. This is, perhaps, transmutation at the atomic level: oceans to mist, to clouds, to rain or snow; mountains to rubble, to mountains again. And we know that some things can have different forms while being the same thing: light as a ray or a particle. Can one thing occupy two spaces at the same time? Can, as with cloning, one genetic code assume two bodies? What is a tomato when made with animal genetic material? These third-millennium mysteries offer us new ways of thinking about what it means to be creatures of spirit and flesh. When are we particles, and when are we rays? What does it mean to have a relationship with God? If matter is good and we are matter, then the kingdom of God within us has something to do with the holy transformation of matter. It becomes possible in our time to think of spirit as matter not yet known or defined by us, rather than to imagine, as in former times, something existing beyond our experience.

Spirit becomes a different order of matter, rather than the opposite of matter. We might want to think about spirit as the matter of chaos that the Creator, and we ourselves, are constantly shaping and transforming. This fundamentally changes how we think about our bodies and the body of creation, how we think about ourselves, our knowledge, and the world and cosmos where we find ourselves. It affects how we think about discovery and invention. If nothing can truly be invented because everything just is, then we are third-millennium alchemists reshaping matter, transmuting it, but not really creating anything new. We are merely creating new ways of seeing what already exists. Is Spirit the void before creation or the motivation behind the universe? Is the essence of God to create, connect, and re-form; to fill the microscopic with the power of the universe, and to make the vastness of the universe a simple reflection of the microscopic? Are we microscopic versions of the Divine — artists and artisans of spirit and matter?

FREEDOM AND RESPONSIBILITY

If we are indeed co-creators with God, the world becomes for us a learning laboratory in which we have considerable freedom, as well as responsibility. The only danger lies in our potential to hurt other parts of creation while we are learning. The only rule is to harm no one and no thing, insofar as we are able. We are not to hurt others to satisfy our curiosity; we are not to damage the world in which others come to growth and learning. We need not abandon scientific research. We can adapt our environment, and ourselves within the environment, but with this caution: what we do must be undertaken with compassion and accountability. This view preserves a respect for life, and acknowledges that other life forms exist independent of human desire and curiosity. It reminds us that we are capable of discerning and choosing the good, and are not necessarily helpless victims of our own technology. It requires a sense of connection and identification with all that exists outside our own egos. Such connection naturally leads to compassion and respect, because we see that in the flower and the lake, in the dog and the rock, we are fundamentally one in origin and quality of goodness.

Learning not only entails the acquisition of knowledge but care in how it is acquired and then applied. One way of viewing scripture is to understand all scripture as a road map or travelogue of human wisdom and experience. This means that one of the holiest aspects of scripture is its revelation of human error and weakness.

A story about the cost of liberation comes from the book of Numbers. The people were wandering in the desert; they were not yet an intentional community, and they were stressed and thirsty. They said to Moses: "Would that we had died when our kindred died before God! Why have you brought the assembly of God into this wilderness for us and our livestock to die here? Why have you brought us up out of Egypt, to bring us to this wretched place? It is no place for grain, or figs, or vines, or pomegranates; and there is no water to drink" [Numbers 20:3–5]. Now what these people needed was water, but what they remembered was a feast. God ensured that they received the water, but no figs or pomegranates. For abundance they would have to work! This is not their first complaint either. In Numbers 11, it was cucumbers, garlic, and onions for which they mourned.

Why was this story recorded? Its purpose is to teach us how an event of great value, a historically dynamic change, can make us yearn for the imagined comforts of the familiar, even if those comforts were fictions and slavery. People tend to mistrust future hope, and have little patience with present trial. Only the past can be safely reinvented to satisfy our memory of the original garden. When we read these accounts and think about our own grumbling, we are encouraged to look with longer vision, to recognize the seeds of hope even in our present difficulties. We learn that to sustain abundance, we must form community, we must behave cooperatively, we must plan and work. The course of Wisdom is humanizing. If we have tasted the fruit of Eden, then we must know that choice has consequences and will set changes in motion — no matter how we choose.

The stories of people whose actions affect and influence the evolution of world history draw us from our self-absorption to a realization of inter-connectedness and responsibility for the whole. We have heard the story of the apostle Peter, who promised never to forsake Jesus but could not stay awake with him, or admit he even knew him, for fear of arrest.[25] What he learned was the cost of discipleship, not as an idea but as a relationship, as a commitment of love and truth, of faithfulness. He came to learn that, once a relationship has formed, its links will forever touch us. He could not truly respond to the invitation to follow Jesus until he had learned how much the relationship would cost his ego and his need for control. How we choose to remember and act on the links of relationship affects how we get on with our lives, how we make sense of our personal histories, what dreams for our future we will let come to be. This consequence of relationship may provide an underpinning for the post-resurrection story in John 21:15–19.

> When they had finished breakfast, Jesus said to Simon Peter, "Simon son of John, do you love me more than these?" He said to him, "Yes, Lord; you know that I love you." Jesus said to him, "Feed my lambs." A second time he said to him, "Simon son of John, do you love me?" He said to him, "Yes, Lord; you know that I love you." Jesus said to him, "Tend my sheep." He said to him the third time, "Simon son of John, do you love me?" Peter felt hurt because he said to him the third time, "Do you love me?" And he said to him, "Lord, you know everything; you know that I love you." Jesus said to him, "Feed my sheep. Very truly, I tell you, when you were younger, you used to fasten your own belt and to go wherever you wished. But when you grow old, you will stretch out your hands, and someone else will fasten a belt around you and take you

where you do not wish to go." (He said this to indicate the kind of death by which he would glorify God.) After this he said to him, "Follow me."

To follow Jesus is to allow ourselves to be immersed in relationship, to voluntarily accept both the pain of connection and the humiliation of our clamouring egos. The stories of human tragedy and sin provide opportunity for our instruction and contemplation. I am not speaking here of a morality that is culturally bound, but of a self-awareness that perceives the far-reaching consequences of our curiosity and selfishness. Conversely, we are invited to see the potential in a sense of connectedness, compassion, and faithfulness.

TRADITION

When we think of learning instead of dogma, whether the dogma is social or religious, then we are neither bound nor justified by earlier ways of thinking. Such openness surpasses the conventions of human society, and places responsibility for the unfolding of the world firmly in human hands. We may not be able to control a volcano, but we can control war. We may be powerless in the face of a monsoon or earthquake, but we can help or hinder the victims of natural disasters. So far, the only disasters we are really inefficient at managing are the ones made by the cyclone of human greed and rage.

And so we hold these biblical stories as precious, not because they are divinely dictated history, but because they help us to look with the long eyes of story, the perspective of the

Divine. These stories are questions inviting us to ponder the mission and mystery of the Divine in its immediate unfolding. When we turn away from the garden of the "golden years," we are able to see the timeless and timely interaction of the human, the Divine, and the cosmic; we recognize the present garden in which we have a task and a challenge again.

We learn as much from the memory of events (tradition) as from the actual events themselves. This is why it is so important to remember the Holocaust and not to let ourselves be misled by those who would minimize that terrible evil of the last century. We want to remember not simply that millions lost their lives, but that every survivor was touched by the experience, in every country and every culture. Humanity learned a new kind of barbarism in World War II — all of us — and we will not be freed from this dreadful knowledge until our basic assumptions about human nature, and the role of the Divine in the world, have profoundly and absolutely shifted. The evil seeds of that war continue to haunt us; this is why we must continue to remember until our pattern of dispute and ideas about entitlement have changed.

When we are grounded in the goodness of this world, and cease to strain for an idealized and intangible fantasy of discorporate life, or for our own perfectibility, then we will treat ourselves and our environment with more respect and with a commitment to *shalom*.

Where then is the place of tradition and the received wisdom of the past? Let us think of tradition as religious recognition, or the organic memory of a culture. Why organic? Because it is never a fixed piece of data. Our past is constantly being re-imagined, re-invented, re-discovered as we change and are changed by circumstance and knowledge. Indeed a criterion for scripture might be — that which must be re-discovered, re-historicized, re-mythologized as the ages pass. The word "remember" suggests putting parts back together, but not necessarily the way they looked before being "dismembered."[26] The body that we knew is the same body, but seen differently, known afresh, having new insight. In this sense, scripture is of divine origin, in that it is never finished until we are finished. It is in a state of constant revelation, as is God. It has potential for renewed investigation over long periods of time, beyond the limits of human cultures and systems.

This organic view suggests that history is an expression of the writer's perception rather than an object isolated from our intervention; that most of the dicta of history are not determinative but derivative of position, perspective, information, and so on. Even sacred scripture has this fluidity and potential. Symbol and ritual actions have similar fluidity. A chalice that Christians use to remind themselves of the sacrifice of Jesus is also an ancient symbol of the womb,[27] blood and water, birth and death, laughter and tears — all held together in one cup, but also in a continuous flow of history and religious experience. Everything that we do is layered with strata of meaning and portent; everything is being shaped, as much as shaping, how we think in the present.

This makes people who need absolutes very uneasy. If the universe is a shifting reality and God can be glimpsed only in hindsight, then how are humans to know what is absolutely and finally true? The answer is that we cannot know anything except the conditional truth of our own experience and of the communities in which we tell our sacred stories. We are thereby both freed from the limits of earlier perceptions and bound by our ties to the stories we must re-member for a contemporary context. Tradition can never function satisfactorily as dogma or legislation; it is bound to a contextual vision rather than a discrete and impartial reality. It is the creation of tradition that we hear in one of the resurrection stories read at Easter.

> Now on that same day two of them were going to a village called Emmaus, about seven miles from Jerusalem, and talking with each other about all these things that had happened. While they were talking and discussing, Jesus himself came near and went with them, but their eyes were kept from recognizing him. And he said to them, "What are you discussing with each other while you walk along?"... Then beginning with Moses and all the prophets, he interpreted to them the things about himself in all the scriptures. As they came near the village to which they were going, he walked ahead as if he were going on. But they urged him strongly, saying, "Stay with us, because it is almost evening and the day is now nearly over." So he went in to stay with them. When he was at the table with them, he took bread, blessed and broke it, and gave it to them. Then their eyes were opened, and they recognized him; and he vanished from their sight. They said to each other, "Were not our hearts burning within us while he was talking to us on the road, while he was opening the scriptures to us?" That same hour they got up and returned to Jerusalem; and they found the eleven and their

companions gathered together. They were saying, "The Lord has risen indeed, and he has appeared to Simon!" Then they told what had happened on the road, and how he had been made known to them in the breaking of the bread.

[Luke 24:13–17, 27–35]

This episode captures the way that the story and remembered experience become ritual and revelation.[28] Not only the word but also the sense of community, at table and at prayer, make it possible to receive revelation and to adjust belief to fit new knowledge. The body of Jesus that had died becomes the body of the community; the body of Jesus that had taught and healed becomes the Spirit of new and continuing revelation, leading those who follow into "all truth," as the gospel of John proclaims. The body of Jesus is remembered in the community of his friends and disciples, who re-discover his life in the process of re-membering his death and his message.

Community is the crucible in which memory meets new experience. Each informs the other; in combination they allow for a continuing revelation and the possibility of new vision. Standing at the crossroads, we are clothed in the Wisdom that we have known, and we welcome the truth that is coming to light. Suddenly we want to accept the invitation of God to see a burning bush, to forget the cucumbers and remember the value of liberation, to plan for a new birth, to give thanks that on a strange and dusty road, in the most improbable places and situations, God is waiting to reveal to us the Divine-self and who we may become.

WISDOM AND CHANGE

Wisdom, like all aspects of God, can neither be possessed nor constrained by our cultures or imaginations. The Spirit will lead us into new truth, and will touch fire in new prophets who will lead us where we would not go, who will demand new choices of us, who will make us suspicious. One of the sayings attributed to Jesus, "See, I am sending you out like sheep into the midst of wolves; so be wise as serpents and innocent as doves" [Matthew 10:16], speaks of the trained consciousness of a Christian. We are invited to learn discernment without abandoning our willingness to see the world through the wondering eyes of a child, to see each thing as newly created, yet to apply all that we have learned to whatever we encounter.

Humanity finds the knowledge of good and evil — wisdom — an irresistible fruit. Choosing is always a question of wisdom, and wisdom always requires choices. The wisdom of Solomon combined the knowledge of many "facts" but also, according to popular memory, Solomon had a canny insight into other humans. In his prayer to God, Solomon asked, "Give your servant therefore an understanding mind to govern your people, able to discern between good and evil; for who can govern this your great people?" [1 Kings 3:9]. The wisdom that is of value has to do with choices, and those choices have ethical and political consequences. To be wise means to accept the limits of what we presently know, to appreciate the depth and breadth of sharing that we are offered through our senses, to use with care the information that we have uncovered or that has been shared with us, and to give thanks through the way we treat others. Our experience of Divinity can be freed, and we can walk deeper into mystery as we expose ourselves to learning, to the desert of dead ends, to the richness of ancient temples, and to the bright wonder of the dawn of another day.

In change, wisdom.

Holy Wisdom, Sophia, Word that is both intention and action, be our guide.
Teach us your Truth, that our experience may be broadened by your insight,
by your gaze across the millennia.
Show us the holiness that began with you and leads us to completion.
Teach us to be slow to know and quick to learn.
Be our gateway and our companion through our lives and in all the world,
may we learn the wisdom of the heart.
Amen.

IN SUFFERING,
WHOLENESS

i am whole and alone
i am partial and in pain
in joy and in pain
we are whole and being completed

The issue of suffering is perhaps one of the most difficult for Christianity. Although we say that creation is good and God is good, suffering seems an ineluctable part of existence. We feel hard-pressed to justify the presence of what appears to be evil in our world. In the crucifixion story, Jesus must endure the jeers of his tormentors seeing God's apparent disregard of his chosen prophet and Jesus' own inability to save himself [Matthew 27:42–44]. In this chapter, I want to suggest that we must come to an acceptance of suffering as an element of our gift of awareness, as material for our understanding, as part of our passage through life and our development as a species. I hope to clarify the difference between existential suffering and suffering as a result of social evil.

WHAT IS SUFFERING?

We are not clear about what actually constitutes suffering; we tend to describe everything from discomfort to agony as suffering. Indeed, what causes one person to suffer grievously may be an incidental discomfort or inconvenience to another. Socially, we have developed an equally unbalanced or distorted perspective. One society is furious that there are no grocery stores in a certain part of town, while another wonders how many of their people will survive a famine. Our news delivery systems, in their competition for popular attention, often blur the distinction between misfortune and tragedy. And many of us may participate in similar distortions when we inadvertently inflate or discount how another perceives pain.

We can say that suffering denotes our experience and understanding of pain. The early Christian stories tell us how much the Romans were impressed by the bravery of the great martyrs, and by their apparent lack of distress, less than would have been expected. We tend to place less emphasis on their pain, and more value on their courage and faith. Pain as the experience of others is minimized, while our own pain is perceived as unconditional and definitive. So pain is personal and subjective.

In *The Body in Pain*, Elaine Scarry says, "For the person in pain, so incontestably and unnegotiably present is it that 'having pain' may come to be thought of as the most vibrant example of what it is to 'have certainty,' while for the other person it is so elusive that 'hearing about pain' may exist as the primary model of what it is 'to have doubt.' Thus pain comes unsharably into our midst as that which cannot be denied and that which cannot be confirmed."[29] Pain separates us into objects for each other and subjects for ourselves. Pain draws us into ourselves and away from others. The pain of others makes us turn away into denial, indifference, or rationalization as we objectify those who are in pain.

As the previous chapter "In Change, Wisdom" suggests, the process of learning, of development, inevitably leads to suffering. But what constitutes suffering? When we have pain, we say we are suffering, and this is true. But is suffering deeper, more elemental than emotional or physical pain? Does suffering derive not only from our being hurt, but also from our awareness of being alone with the hurt? For me, this broader, deeper notion of suffering provides a key to understanding the human condition. We know that touch and sympathetic support have tremendous power to ease pain. So is suffering perhaps the experience of alienation, of being left alone with whatever pain we are experiencing? Is suffering a sense of what it means to be totally abandoned in the universe, an awareness of disconnection from all that is good? When people are deep in mourning, they speak about the greyness of grief, the absence of colour or music in their lives.

Our suffering, then, has something to do with "disconnection." We know that the most devastating suffering involves torture and humiliation, pain and alienation, together. Pain alone would not constitute suffering. Alienation added to pain results in suffering. Any of us who spend time in hospitals will remember that those patients who experience love, support, and sharing with others seem able to deal with their pain in more creative, less alienated and alienating, ways. They will perhaps say that they are having pain, but they will rarely describe it as suffering. Those who have a sense of disconnection from others, whether this is observably true, will describe themselves as suffering. Those with conditions that impede or prevent communication seem much more difficult to comfort. They appear to us to "suffer" more, although their physical pain may be no greater.

The story of the garden of Gethsemane provides a compelling example of how compassion, integrity, goodness, can lead to suffering. Jesus prayed to God for release from the dread or inevitability of his death, but God was silent. Even his companions abandoned him and slept, while he wrestled with anguish and terror. In Luke's account, an angel comes to strengthen him, but even this only makes him "pray more earnestly." In the face of great suffering, there is only silence, the dark valley where the soul confronts itself in isolation.

> He came out and went, as was his custom, to the Mount of Olives; and the disciples followed him. When he reached the place, he said to them, "Pray that you may not come into the time of trial." Then he withdrew from them about a stone's throw, knelt down, and prayed, "Father, if you are willing, remove this cup from me; yet, not my will but yours be done." Then an angel from heaven appeared to him and gave him strength. In his anguish he prayed more earnestly, and his sweat became like great drops of blood falling down on the ground. When he got up from prayer, he came to the disciples and found them sleeping because of grief, and he said to them, "Why are you sleeping? Get up and pray that you may not come into the time of trial."
>
> [Luke 22:39–46]

In this vivid snapshot, the gospel writer is showing us how the Christ "suffered." We are told not only that Jesus was beaten and killed, but also that he knew stark fear and abandonment. This feeling of abandonment rings throughout all stories of suffering. Anyone who has visited victims in war-torn countries or refugee camps, and has asked what they need, has heard the haunting refrain: "Do not forget us; do not abandon us in your hearts; even if you can do nothing concrete for us, do not forget us." Some of the grief of the chronically ill and the very elderly derives from the fear that they have been forgotten. In the psalms, we read about God caring for Israel: "He has remembered his steadfast love and faithfulness to the house of Israel" [Psalm 98:3]; or about God seeming to abandon the people: "Why do you forget our affliction and oppression? " [Psalm 44:24].

I would suggest that all suffering — physical, emotional, or mental; personal or social; or their combinations — arises from a sense of being alone in the struggle. Like depression, suffering tends to be self-reinforcing. Once the cycle of suffering has begun, it is difficult to break. We become habituated to suffering and its causes, like poverty and war. Being inured to such conditions, we are virtually paralyzed and cannot act to save ourselves. When preoccupied with suffering, we often become irritated by anyone who attempts to break through our isolation; we insist that no one has ever suffered like this before, and no one can possibly understand. In social terms, we reject efforts to ameliorate situations of pain, resigning ourselves to evil as an essential condition of life. There is no reason whatsoever why the world could not choose tomorrow to abjure war and struggle to eliminate the worst ravages of poverty. But addiction to violence and greed has locked us into a cycle of suffering that we know will touch every nation sooner or later, and destroy each meadow and city.

We also know that to allow anyone to enter the circle of our pain will immediately begin to heal the pain. Comfort can be extended only to the willing heart. Socially, we know that the only thing standing between us and a peaceful world, where children grow up without fear or hunger, is the common will to change — in other words, wisdom. But this will require energy and vision. It will call us to awaken, to give up our deathly sleepiness in the face of suffering. It will force us to exchange our dependence on an intervening God for a partnership with an encouraging God, who has given us the world and the power to act.

So here are the aspects of suffering as I am exploring it. There is some kind of loss: physical integrity, personal control, identity, relationship. There is some kind of pain: social, emotional, physical. There is some form of isolation and alienation: imprisonment, depression, disability. Each aspect leads to suffering only when we recognize and acknowledge it.

LOVE AND SUFFERING

We all know that to love another inevitably leads to hurt and loss, regardless of the vitality of the relationship. One way or another, all of us will be hurt by those we love, or we will visit hurt upon them, inadvertently or deliberately. Some of us accept this inevitable loss as the price we pay for the benefit of love, even if it seems cruel and unnecessary. Others of us feel a sense of betrayal that, whether we will it or not, we must participate in this cosmic reality.

Another side of this feeling of loss is rejection, which tends to be experienced as intentional abandonment. This begins early in life for us. We are born alone — even twins who have shared a womb. At our birth, we are separated immediately from the one being with whom we have shared existence. This imposed isolation is the first out-of-the-womb experience we know. It is so wrenching that we spend most of the rest of our lives attempting to avoid experiencing it again. Even before we can understand the reason, we may interpret every denial, every dismissal to bed, as a rejection, perhaps as a memory of our birth.

Later on, usually in adolescence, most of us are hurt by the end of "first love." Attempting to diminish its pain in hindsight, we often call it "puppy love." But I would suggest that it is perhaps one of the deepest pains of self-initiated relationship that we will ever feel. For many of us, it is the first time we can verbalize the loss, the first time we can appreciate the cost of love. And because it is minimized, we do feel isolated. Such pain is most traumatic to our social selves. We learn not only that others can reject us, but that they do not respect our feelings, and that we ourselves perhaps should not take them so seriously.

Falling in love is learning how to give up what we cling to most vigorously. As a spiritual discipline, it means accepting change, the death of old ideas, old experiences. Jesus tells Mary in the garden not to cling to him, and after his death he is known in new ways and through new people. The love and devotion had not died, but they were transformed and understood in different ways. This is resurrection — all that we have experienced so vibrantly will be experienced again, but differently. St. Paul tells us how the resurrected body differs from the physical body [1 Corinthians 15:37– 41]; but this is metaphor for a deeper truth — to love is to release both our future expectations and our past experience to the refining power of loss, so that we might have renewed life.

I suspect that we minimize the sting of love because we want to pack it away rather than learn from its power and intensity. We resist learning that hurt is normal, a constant reality of creation, not an unhappy accident in the otherwise serene progress of the universe. To be hurt means that we will suffer loss, isolation, and fear. Risking in love, learning from rejection, discovering our strength in the face of suffering, are all part of our training for life. This training is of critical importance for those who say that we follow the way of the cross, because we must remain vulnerable to being irredeemably wounded by suffering.

SUFFERING AND DEVELOPMENT

If suffering is so normal that it conditions us from our first breath, and if avoiding it is clearly impossible, then how are we to deal with suffering? In the second creation story, the problem of isolation is addressed. God looks at the human creature who has been made and says, "It is not good that the *adamah* should be alone; I will make a helper to be a partner" [Genesis 2:19]. Then its new partner leads the creature to bite on the fruit of self-awareness, and a relationship is born. This is the corollary — no self-awareness, no relationship. To develop relationship, we must first have a sense of self. Indeed, the creature has only a rudimentary sense of God before eating the fruit. To grow up is to become self-aware; to become self-aware is to learn about separation; to learn about separation is to know suffering.

Why does suffering exist? Because the route to development lies through the path of self-awareness to affiliation, to disentanglement, to interrelationship. We must become aware of our separate selves, then we must learn to attach ourselves to another. Then again, we must learn autonomy of thought and action. In the final stage, we must learn to coexist in an interdependent and mutually beneficial manner. If a butterfly that lives for only a day has an important place in the universe, then we, who are only relatively less ephemeral, have a place also. Everything we do hastens or hinders the growth of love in the universe. Every hidden thought, every spoken word, every committed act, either contributes to the well-being and healing of the cosmos, or erodes the fabric of creation. Where we place our suffering, and in what service, is of cosmic importance.

Jesus tells us that the kingdom of God is within. We can most deeply touch and learn from whatever is inside our own lives and our associations with other people. The kingdom of God within is in process, unfinished, open-ended. We need not cling to the past, because the Spirit is encouraging us to a wider picture in each moment. Jesus lives out this teaching first by loving and calling a familial association around himself, and then by leaving it to develop its own life and form. Jesus as a historical figure, and Jesus as an object of faith, are still being revealed as we deepen our experience and learn from him in each era of the church's life. As we change, our picture of Jesus changes also. As we develop broader understandings and sensibilities, we become less afraid of differences and endings, and more curious about next steps in faith.

SUFFERING, GROWTH, AND LOVE

And why do we want to develop anyway, either as a species or as individuals? What's wrong with the lives and the boundaries we have? It might depend on my location and perspective, but it seems to me that everywhere we look in our world, we see hurt to be healed, progress to be altered, relationships to be mended. The human endeavour can hardly claim to be complete. Christians speak of growing into Christ, gaining a transformed body like the body of Christ, being one with the Creator the way Christ is one, becoming complete and fulfilled as the Creator is complete and fulfilled. A significant feature of Christianity is its impulse for growth and change, for acknowledging that everything is in the process of transformation.

The pathway of human development as individuals, cultures, and as a species requires love and suffering because it is through the experience of alienation that we come to value association, not only for ourselves but for each person and society. Love and suffering accompany each other because they condition each other. To remember that no beloved can be held forever is to acknowledge the fragility and precious nature of the beloved — we experience anticipated suffering. To be hurt through love is to know the power of suffering, not only to isolate us but also to bring us through to a new understanding, a new way of seeing ourselves and the beloved whose relationship with us has been altered. Suffering is the way we learn to share life, the way we learn both to differentiate ourselves from others and to reattach ourselves to others through compassion and love.

When we understand the life of the Spirit as being constantly reshaped by separation and reunion, then the presence of suffering becomes comprehensible, even if painful. Religious people who have developed a method of prayer and reflection rarely find themselves with an ongoing sense of abandonment or psychic suffering.

Dietrich Bonhoeffer found that memorizing the psalms helped him to endure imprisonment. His love for his compatriots, for his sinful nation and the Jewish victims, spun him back into the hands of his oppressors who would ultimately kill him as a traitor. He suffered not because he knew abandonment, but because he felt safe while others suffered and were killed. He could not permit either the oppressors or the victims to be alone in their respective sin or martyrdom, and so he renounced personal safety for solidarity with others, for integrity and love. His personal suffering, derived from his participation in the suffering of others, was in turn mitigated by his sense of community both with others and the Divine.

> Every act of self-control of the Christian is also a service to the fellowship. On the other hand, there is no sin in thought, word, or deed, no matter how personal or secret, that does not inflict injury upon the whole fellowship. An element of sickness gets into the body; perhaps nobody knows where it comes from or in what member it has lodged, but the body is infected. This is the proper metaphor for the Christian community. We are members of a body, not only when we choose to be, but in our whole existence. Every member serves the whole body, either in its

health or to its destruction. This is no mere theory; it is a
spiritual reality.[30]

Suffering for Others

When we believe that our own seemingly modest actions
have significance and power in the world, we are empow-
ered to undertake what appears to be suffering for the love
of others. This kind of sacrificial love has nothing to do with
masochism. It always has to do with an unswerving sense of
empathy. When we read about the great martyrs, we see that
they hoped for their lives up to the end. Equally, they sought
to lead or inspire others at most, and at least they chose one
pain (love) for a less satisfactory pain (alienation, non-par-
ticipation). They are witnesses to an outcome that they
themselves can experience only through the eyes of hope and
not in their mortal lives. Pictures of the victims of war are
important, not for the sensationalism that attends them but
for the living reminder that we could be they, that no one is
guaranteed exemption from this price in the world in which
we live.

Suffering is the centre of the cross. It is the nexus of love
and alienation, life and death, anomie and meaning, abandonment and fulfillment. The centre of the cross is the point
where the contradictions meet; it is the *chairotic* moment of
insight in which the paradoxes that haunt us finally make
sense. At the centre of the cross, we are, everyone of us, per-
secutor and victim, witness and perpetrator, child and mature
person. At the centre of the cross, we are complete and yet

we are becoming. At the centre of the cross, we observe a man who becomes a god for us, who transcends both his life and death to call us to a deeper understanding of the hope with which we are to live, the vision we are to hold before our eyes.

Jesus says that those who want to save their lives need to learn how to give them up. At the moment when the contradictions are resolved, we see that we never have really had our lives, but that by spending them, using them, we can create meaning and make a place for ourselves in the history of the world. We may be servants in the house of the Holy One, but without our small sacrifice, without our small lives and offerings, the whole world would be poorer, our development would be more arduous, and our release would be more prolonged. In this moment, we understand our personal deaths not as wrongs but as completions, fulfillments of the tasks we have undertaken to ease the suffering of others by our love and vision of hope.

In speaking of death, Thomas Merton notes, "Hence, life 'dies' to itself in order to give itself away, and thus affirms itself more maturely, more fruitfully, and more completely. We live in order to die to ourselves and give everything to others. Such dying is the fruit of life, the evidence of mature and productive living. It is, in fact, the end or goal of life."[31] Merton is suggesting a life focused not on death but on others, and on the spaces in their lives where suffering exists. When we are totally immersed in love of life and of living creatures, our own deaths are almost incidental beside the wonder that we feel and the compassion that moves us to action and to prayer.

To step into the place where others suffer, to open ourselves to the pain of loss and abandonment, is to accept that
we all participate in the painful delivery of the created order. Each one of us a womb and the product of a womb, each
life sown in tears and joyful release. The apocalyptic imagery
that presages a new order — however one may choose to
think about what that order means — suggests the pain of
labour: "When you hear of wars and rumours of wars, do
not be alarmed; this must take place, but the end is still to
come. For nation will rise against nation, and kingdom
against kingdom; there will be earthquakes in various places;
there will be famines. This is but the beginning of the birthpangs" [Mark 13:7–8]. One would be hard-pressed to find a
time when this description did not accurately portray reality somewhere in the world. We might want to speculate
that the unfolding of life on this planet, and of human
civilization in particular, requires a continual birthing of consciousness, and we see this reflected in the created order as
well as in our societies.

GOD, CHRIST, AND SUFFERING

This prolonged apocalypse is mirrored in the ongoing inser-
tion of Christ into the world — not an event so much as a
process, a second coming into the world. Simultaneously the
world is being bent in suffering, and being healed and
renewed. Elaine Scarry speaks of this as God being both omnipotent and vulnerable, sentient and wounded, God as both
the subject and object of human suffering. "It is not that the

concept of power is eliminated; it is certainly not that the idea of suffering is eliminated; it is that the earlier relation between them is eliminated. They are no longer manifestations of each other; one person's pain is not the sign of another person's power. The greatness of human vulnerability is not the greatness of divine invulnerability. They are unrelated and therefore can occur together: God is both omnipotent and in pain."[32] On the cross, Jesus connects the holiness and power of God to the suffering of the world. To "take up our cross" as the church is to stand at that centre where the only power that matters is the power of loving relationship.

God is both beyond the human condition and enmeshed in it, and more; for God is also incarnate in the whole created order, "groaning in labour." So we say that the Spirit groans with us, labours with us to deliver us. The cosmos is both the divine child and the body of the Great Mother who wills life and growth for all her children. Jesus, then, is not only the incarnation but also the revelation of the whole incarnation, of Spirit becoming known and revealed in matter. Jesus the person conveys the Spirit with power and wisdom to create a new order, a new consciousness. We are invited to be born of Spirit, to experience the fire and breath of holiness flashing through our lives. It is Jesus who has taught us not to fear the power of flame and whirlwind but to be caught up in it, to become like him in daring and passion.

This aspect of the incarnation, the extended passion of Christ that can be seen throughout most Christian writing, canonical and otherwise, is expressed in every event of his life, from his feasting at table to his sorrow over Lazarus. To be incarnate means, in a Christian context, to participate in the suffering of the world through the circumstances of one's own life. This pushes our ideas about suffering into the realm of paradox. For if everyone suffers, then suffering is both an isolating experience and the single common experience of every human brought into the world. To suffer means to feel loss and abandonment, yet in loss and abandonment we are most in solidarity with all that is, that has been, and that is to come. Indeed, through each experience of suffering, every one of us participates in the suffering of Christ and thereby gains both the potential and the hope of resurrection, of understanding embodiment in broader and more enriching ways, and of seeing ourselves not just as dust, but as cosmic dust alive with a purpose and a place.

TAKING OUR PLACE IN THE STORY

For suffering to change, in our understanding, from a regrettable error in the divine plan, or a continued punishment for growing up, to a difficult but essential part of human development, we need to distinguish between suffering that is "natural" and suffering that we impose in our lust for divine power. Since God, the source of life and death, the Alpha and Omega, is our ultimate image of power, we tend to feel powerful only when we have the potential to give life or cause harm. Not surprisingly, the people who most capture our imaginations are either healers or killers.[33]

When we think of being made in the image of God, we tend to fantasize about power, rather than birthing and self-giving love, as being most godlike. This stems from our failure to recognize ourselves not as beginners or enders, but as continuers in the action of the cosmos. We are not powerful enough to truly create anything from nothing; nor can we utterly destroy matter, although we can bend it and re-shape it. We are caught in the midst of a cosmic drama and invited to write the parts for ourselves. The image of God that most closely approximates the potential of our human condition is the story of Jesus — the one who makes relationships of healing, honesty, and self-giving love.

In one sense, the garden gate is closed. We cannot return to a state of ignorance and unknowing without destroying ourselves as a species. One might interpret some of our more horrific technologies as wish fulfillments for a return to the womb through our own annihilation. As we contaminate our air, land, and water, we are gradually remaking the world to be unliveable. In this way, we will recreate the garden indeed. This time, however, it will not be a nursery, but a tomb. What was initially the ignorance of pre-consciousness will become the ignorance of non-being.

> Every day I call on you, O God;
> I spread out my hands to you.
> Do you work wonders for the dead?
> Do the shades rise up to praise you?
> Is your steadfast love declared in the grave,
> or your faithfulness in Abaddon?
> Are your wonders known in the darkness,
> or your saving help in the land of forgetfulness?
> [Psalm 88:9–12]

To grow up as a species means to accept the burden of consciousness that inevitably involves awareness of loss and abandonment — suffering. But there are still choices for us to make. We can decide where we would place our energies — in the creation of suffering or in healing, in learning through suffering or in denial; in solidarity with the community of suffering or in isolation and self-absorption. Suffering is both opportunity and curse for us. We can hold it as a weapon or as a doorway to new life. We can be monsters or angels, and sometimes both at the same time.

The world has been given to humans to "have dominion" in, and we have choices about how we will walk through this garden of the world. Whether we destroy our garden, break our toys, and kill our friends, depends on how we come to understand suffering. Suffering that is neither sought nor administered but experienced, endured, and used for the growth of wisdom, can be our rite of passage to a new way of being human, a way exemplified by Jesus, an incarnation of God's compassion and woundedness. As long as we confuse the suffering that gives us birth with the suffering that we visit upon each other to feel like gods, then we will make our lives, and the life of the planet, a misery.

If the whole of creation is suffering birthpangs, then the whole of creation is also dying and being remade, second by second, as one star goes supernova and another galaxy is born. We do not need to fear this. When we understand that we are participants in the evolution of the universe, not gods or victims, then we can greet both pain and healing as cosmic moments, and see ourselves with all creation as partners in the unfolding, the development, the mystery, the revelation. Science then becomes not the laboratory of dangerous experiment, but a place of holiness and discovery of the Divine, just as Roger Bacon once believed.[34] Science is the revelation of divine mystery. And we are not mad dabblers but reverent, wisdom-seeking, compassionate explorers of existence.

Our suffering connects us to each other and to the whole unfolding of creation, and also distinguishes us one from another. Like a blizzard, we are each a snowflake, but from the scope of history, a blur of precipitation. A children's hymn, which as a child I found highly debatable, tells us that God sees the little sparrow fall and has even more concern for humans. As I speculated on how many dead birds I had witnessed, I found this sentiment of dubious comfort. Perhaps the focus is skewed, however. We would rather say that, in creating us, God also witnesses our existence. In the memory of God, we live, rather than "have lived" or "will live," forever. As each creature comes into existence, rather than as each creature dies, it is recognized as part of the fabric of the Divine, and as a separate being. If we say that the Divine transcends time, and that we are carved in the palm of that existence [Isaiah 49:14–16], then our existence is tied and bound to the Holy One.

But Zion said, "The Holy One has forsaken me,
my God has forgotten me."
Can a woman forget her nursing child,
or show no compassion for the child of her womb?

Even these may forget,
yet I will not forget you.
See, I have inscribed you on the palms of my hands;
your walls are continually before me.

Once we live, we live forever as part of God. For humans, this suggests that our consciousness participates in the unfolding and recording of all that exists, in suffering and thanksgiving. Becoming is painful; birth is painful. Beyond the labour is joy; beyond our human emotions is Life in all its fullness.

Merton said, "Faith gives us life in Christ…. To accept this is impossible unless one has profound hope in the incomprehensible fruitfulness that emerges from this dissolution of our ego in the ground of being and of Love. Such a hope is not the product of human reason, it is a secret gift of grace…. We accept our emptying because we realize that our very emptiness is fulfillment and plenitude. In our emptiness the one Word is clearly spoken. It says, 'I will never let go of you or desert you' [Hebrews 13:5], for I am your God and I am Love."[35]

In suffering, wholeness.
Beloved of God, you shared human life with us.
You knew laughter and tears, courage and fear.
Still our trembling souls that we may see you before us,
a light to guide our feet and a comfort on our journey.
Show us how to be companions to others that we may be
bound ever closer to you and to your Way.

Holy Jesus, child of God and of Mary,
be our friend and brother that we may walk through storms
and sunshine with your name on our lips
and your message in our actions.
Amen.

IN REPENTANCE, COMPASSION

you create me and so i live
an oak of consciousness
you uncreate me and so i live
a ray of light
you create me

THE TRADITION OF GUILT AND SHAME

From the Judeo-Christian tradition, we carry an ancestral pseudo-memory about repentance that suggests guilt and shame. This memory has its origins in the traditional interpretations of the story of the garden of Eden. As formed in us, this story involves disobedience and indelible error, redeemable only through human blood, the sacrifice we have come to associate with the death of Christ. As a result, we feel that some extraordinary penance is necessary if we are to avoid punishment for trespasses that are either intentional or inadvertent. For us to become more fully the people of Christ in this time, we must examine what we have meant by repentance and what we could mean. We need to move to a creative understanding rather than the isolating idea of shame that has dominated much of our thinking about matters spiritual and ethical. Shame distracts us from the light of truth, separates us from one another, interferes with healing and new life. It is more than time for us to liberate ourselves from shame and exchange shame for responsibility.

Shame is closely allied to grief. Through shame we have often made sense of our pain, our sense of being exiles from the love of God. Indeed, the external expressions of penitence look much like those of grief.

> O God, do not rebuke me in your anger,
> or discipline me in your wrath.
> For your arrows have sunk into me,
> and your hand has come down on me.

For my iniquities have gone over my head;
they weigh like a burden too heavy for me.

O God, all my longing is known to you;
my sighing is not hidden from you.
My heart throbs, my strength fails me;
as for the light of my eyes — it also has gone from me.

But I am like the deaf, I do not hear;
like the mute, who cannot speak.
Truly, I am like one who does not hear,
and in whose mouth is no retort.

For I am ready to fall,
and my pain is ever with me.
I confess my iniquity;
I am sorry for my sin.
[Psalm 38:1–2, 4, 9–10, 13–14, 17–18]

The emphasis in this psalm, as in many other expressions of penitence, is on the humiliation of the penitent and on the graciousness of God to forgive. All misfortune is understood as the result of iniquity or, at the very least, inattention to the demands of the faith.

One of the most painful experiences I had in hospital chaplaincy was helping people whose loved ones, babies in particular, had died. Their pain arose not so much from the death, although that was deeply sad, as from the feeling that they were at fault somehow, and that death was the consequence. One young couple asked me if their baby had died because of their common-law relationship; another couple confessed that they had not been in church for a long time, and that this was perhaps a message. Our "folk" wisdom tells us that misfortune is a direct consequence of actions that displease the God of rewards and punishments. This idea still has such currency that innocent suffering cannot be explained easily, and the prosperity of the rich sinner is seen as an injustice on the part of God. The story of Dives and Lazarus in the afterlife [Luke 16:19ff] shows how we make sense of the good fortune of the selfish or wicked — they will be punished in the end!

This is not new thinking, but it becomes less and less helpful, as we proposed in the previous chapter, "In Suffering, Wholeness." Actually, repentance understood as punitive humiliation for wickedness in "thought, word and deed" is so unpleasant that either we avoid it completely, or we dwell on it with unhealthy morbidity. Much of the self-mockery of those who do feel shame derives from an acquired sense of unworthiness and an internalized need for punishment.

One of the most poorly attended services of the church is the Good Friday rite, in which we remember either the courage and love of Jesus or his atonement to God for the sins of humanity, for our failure. Some of our discomfort comes from our powerlessness before an accusation that is larger than a single human life. Most of our discomfort comes from being blamed and having to propitiate an angry and demanding God, who has yet to forgive humanity for being who we were made to be. This God required the blood sacrifice of Jesus, but we continue to be held responsible, even when we try to slough off some guilt onto others — Romans, Jews — to ease the spiritual pressure. Good Friday is often experienced as a lose-lose situation — we cannot be saved without Jesus' death, but we must also be blamed for his death.

An Act of Responsible Beings

We need to separate repentance and suffering, and to disentangle our ideas of reward and punishment. Repentance is the cry of the Hebrew prophets, of John the Baptist, and, to a lesser degree, of Jesus.[36] In Hebrew, the two common words for the verb to repent mean either to go back, to turn from one position to another (*shuwb*), or to feel remorse, to sigh (*nacham*). In Greek, the word *metanoia* means to turn around and move in a different direction. Hair shirts, wailing, and torn scalps notwithstanding, repentance is not so much about guilt as about awareness and empathy — awareness of having taken a wrong direction, and empathy with those affected by our actions. In other words, repentance arises from insight into the consequences of our behaviour toward another, and from identification with the suffering in the life of another.

As a result of this kind of thinking, the geometry changes. There is now no triangulation; God does not intervene between parties to mete out consequences. The situation and its resolution, or the tragedy, lies in human hands. God does not wave the wand of punishment or prosperity. The world and its peoples are our responsibility. Jesus dies because he is fully human, because people of integrity live dangerously in situations of oppression. Jesus dies not so much *for* us as *with* us, in our struggle to be free and aware. Jesus suffers in solidarity with humanity, not simply because of humanity. We can choose either to engage suffering in solidarity, like Jesus, or to exacerbate suffering by our actions or indifference.

What about our couples with their babies? Guilt has nothing to do with them. They need to know that their actions have not brought about the death of their children, that God wanted these babies to live and prosper as much as they did. They need to know that the connection between their children's death and the Holy One exists only in God's compassionate love, which permits death when suffering is, or may be, too extreme. They need to hear that God is their consolation and comfort — not the One who takes away, but the One who receives; not the One who punishes, but the One who forgives; not the One who yells, but the One who weeps. They do not need to repent; *the church* needs to repent if we will not stand with them in their suffering.

THE WAY TO LIFE AND GROWTH FOR THE SINNER

If suffering belongs not so much to events as to our response to, and definition of, certain experiences (as seen in the chapter "In Suffering, Wholeness"), then why be concerned with the suffering of another? Why not leave them to their misery and deal with our own — the "look after number one" ethic? The answer is that, inevitably, suffering will become a shared experience; suffering is part of the price of awareness, of being conscious participants, responsible actors, in the growth of the universe toward goodness.

If sin has been involved in causing suffering, we are all both victim and perpetrator, caught up in the systemic nature of evil, which denies life and growth. Sin is a condition in which we find ourselves on the side of selfish power and oppression, rather than on the side of helping and healing. Sin means holding the gun, withholding the food, causing the pain. If we have been complicit with those who have caused suffering, it will be delivered to our door in a package that cannot be refuted. Jesus promises that those who are persecutors will be known by their deeds. "So have no fear of them; for nothing is covered up that will not be uncovered, and nothing secret that will not become known. What I say to you in the dark, tell in the light; and what you hear whispered, proclaim from the housetops" [Matthew 10:26–27].

This is wonderful news for those whose oppression has been hidden, and also for those who need to be redeemed from their selfish, evil ways (whether they like it or not), so that they may participate again in life and growth. This is the message of the historical punishment of sin, "unto the third and fourth generation of those who hate me" — the vulnerable will be avenged; perhaps not individually but collectively, there will be an accounting. Until there is, the sin will continue to haunt and blemish for succeeding generations.

If suffering is a consequence of sin, then repentance is the corrective measure to redeem the sinner, when he or she returns to the side of the suffering in an act of solidarity, understanding, and healing, and thereby enables a growing holiness and wholeness. This message of repentance comes to us, then, as good news — where we have erred, we will be corrected; and where we have been sinned against, we will ultimately be vindicated. All things return to the primary value that is goodness; evil is transitory and cannot withstand the urge to be reborn into wholeness. This is the judgement and the deliverance of the societies and cultures of all times.

ACCEPTING OUR SUFFERING

At an individual level, we are invited to a different perception of reality. When we see another suffering, we are able to connect to our own sense of alienation, the isolating quality of our own pain. We have seen that, as we move through our suffering, we come to recognize how we are part of the labour, the whole unfolding, of creation. Both the healing of suffering, and the momentum to pass through the tunnel of pain, require a recognition of the way that suffering has brought us back into community, the way that alienation itself has returned us to our sense of belonging. We are reintegrated into community, but there is one difference — we will never again see others as intact, invulnerable; we will see all of creation, and particularly other humans, as contingent, friable, delicate, yet ultimately resilient and filled with potential.

When we see ourselves as participants in the health and healing of the world, we see ourselves as part of the problem as well. To accept repentance as good news means to acknowledge our own pain, isolation, and helplessness before the enormous complexity of the systems we have created. We come to understand that, in this web of life, we are all caught in the moment of choosing the apple and experiencing the consequent awareness.

As Susan Griffin remarks in *The Eros of Everyday Life*,

> Yet the communion is here. Even as I touch my hand to my face I can feel it. That radiant love that is an undeniable part of the body. What June Jordan calls an "intelligent love." Seeking to see, to know, to take in all that is, as it is. To meet all that exists. It is by such a sacrament that wounds will heal us. Any healing will require us to witness all our histories where they converge, the history of empires and emancipations, of slave ships as well as underground railroads; it requires us to listen back into the muted cries of the beaten, the burned, the forgotten and also to hear the ring of speech among us, meeting the miracle of that. And if we weep in the apprehension, let us take the capacity to weep and marvel as proof of a wisdom in the stuff of our existence, at one with the redwood forests … as it is with the watery cells of our own bodies, or the star, just bursting into a distant brightness. Our sorrow and joy belong to this history, have evolved from the cooling planet of earth…. The tears and laughter with which we meet this moment are as much a part of intelligence as any reason and can move us deeper to the core of things.[37]

And thus we are called to repentance, to turn to a new way

of seeing the world — another chance for ourselves, a new set of responsibilities. Mother Teresa used to say that she loved the poor, and could take on even the most extreme physical challenges, because she could see Christ in the face of the suffering. But maybe we need to see our own face in the face of suffering. Maybe we need to recognize the pain that we all carry, whether lightly or as burdens, the hurt that we would avoid at all costs in our own lives. To have this interior knowledge of pain is to offer healing when we spot it in others. Jorge Luis Borges wrote, "Perhaps a feature of the crucified face lurks in every mirror; perhaps the face died, or was erased, so that God may be all of us. "[38]

Jesus discovers in the garden that, despite the fear and grief that make his friends unreliable, he must walk into his commitment to healing and risk his own security, his own body. We choose to walk back into sharing pain, because we would not wish another to tread the path of suffering alone. Moreover, as we become seasoned veterans of repentance, acknowledging both our sin and the pain that we carry, it becomes easier to reach out to others, and easier to accept the healing of our own souls.

RESISTING PRINCIPALITIES AND POWERS

There is a rather funny healing story in the gospel of John [chapter 9], in which Jesus cures the sight of a young man who has been blind since birth. Although this man can evidently see and his whole life is changed, the people refuse to believe it; they say it is impossible because of his sin, his ancestors' sin, or Jesus' sin. None of their objections has real validity, as anyone familiar with the breadth of Torah would probably have known. But it is true that, when blindness changes to sight, when isolation resolves into belonging, nothing is ever the same again. This young man is not a miracle but a threat because he can see and, in seeing, he can move from his own blindness to affecting the blindness of others.

The world can be changed and is changed all the time by people who repent, who turn from blindness to sight, from apathy to action, from indifference to faith. Quite correctly, the powers and principalities of the world fear this healing because it suggests that poverty, war, oppression, and all other political and culturally imposed pain can be eradicated, healed by clear vision. You cannot lie to a person who sees clearly; you cannot deceive someone who has been given wise eyes. A nation of mostly wise eyes would choose differently, would have different expectations of its officials. And then the powers and principalities would have to manage and facilitate generosity and sharing, rather than manipulate minds and information.

I am speaking of how we become unwitting cogs in political machinery that cannot succeed because it will not recognize suffering and repentance as political processes, evidencing great harm but carrying potential for great good. Unfortunately, profit-making has been confused with government, and manipulation of citizens with humble service. As long as we allow ourselves to be cocooned from repentance, we will not be healed; we will not learn compassion. We will be like those who may "indeed look, but not perceive, and may indeed listen, but not understand" [Mark 4:12].

CONFRONTING OUR INNER MONSTERS

The whole question of compassion and forgiveness is fraught with difficulty, but I would suggest that it is impossible to forgive until we recognize our own need for forgiveness. Until we each acknowledge our own potential to cause great harm, we cannot forgive the potential or actuality in others, and so we cannot heal it. We cannot feel compassion until we have experienced in ourselves the need for forgiveness.

One of the most difficult challenges for each human being is to see in oneself the monsters that we project onto others. We must each ask ourselves in what circumstances we might become the molester, the murderer, the liar, the drug dealer, the terrorist. It is not sufficient to say, "Never me!" In our world, these are categories and labels rather than people. And it is no longer true, if it ever was, that people are innocent until found guilty. The second a person is arrested for crime, we are ready with judgement and noose, and often feel cheated if somehow the person is found innocent. And we incite the victims to a sense of righteous vengeance, although we know that retribution may be more difficult to heal than the initial violation. Such rage allows us to hide ourselves, our complicity, our fear about the monster within.

This systemic lust for retribution exposes alienation at its heart. The attendant pain and despair we treat as disease, rather than as a way of experiencing the world at a particular moment in time. There is nothing inherently evil in pain or despair; they can be passages to a new way of seeing the world, of receiving healing. But such healing will not happen until people look deep within, to learn to love their inner monsters and their potential. It is only compassion that tames the beast, only love that turns a sword into a tool. To have peace in ourselves is to accept the monsters within, to love them until they become responsive and beautiful. This is the ministry of Jesus — to love even the monsters, to defend the vulnerable, to tell the truth, to show us ourselves, to tell us how we are loved because of and despite ourselves. Through Jesus, we are able to understand God as a good and loving parent who weeps over some of the paths we take, but who cannot resist our appeal. We are connected to our Maker with the umbilical cord of light and spirit and passion. From Jeremiah 31:18–20, we read,

Indeed I heard Ephraim pleading:
"You disciplined me, and I took the discipline;
I was like a calf untrained.
Bring me back, let me come back,
for you are my God.
For after I had turned away I repented;
and after I was discovered, I struck my thigh;
I was ashamed, and I was dismayed
because I bore the disgrace of my youth."

Is Ephraim my dear son?
Is he the child I delight in?
As often as I speak against him,
I still remember him.
Therefore I am deeply moved for him;
I will surely have mercy on him,
says the Holy One.

RECOGNIZING HOW WE AFFECT OTHERS

Repentance begins by wondering at the way our actions affect others. This does not mean a kind of gentle dishonesty, but rather an engaged honesty — "my small truth" spoken with compassion. In repentance there are no big truths, only little truths that we glean for ourselves as we walk the path. Repentance is recognizing the extent of our power and the limitation of our wisdom. Remorse is always accompanied by humility, as we compare the effect of our action to the satisfaction it brought, even if the action was motivated by a political sense of righteousness.

In a novel I was reading, a young thief steals a rich girl's jewellery — that is his occupation. But as he leaves the room, he notices that her nakedness is partly revealed. He finds this both disturbing and compelling as he escapes. What he learns from this experience is how, in stealing, he is robbing people not just of their possessions but of their sense of privacy and security. "Crokus shared something of ... sardonic reserve for the pretence [of the wealthy]. Adding fuel to this fire was a healthy dose of youthful resentment towards anything that smacked of authority .... yet he'd never before understood the most subtle and hurtful insult his thefts delivered — the invasion and violation of privacy.... Eventually, Crokus grasped that the vision had everything to do with — everything. He'd come into her room, a place where ... innocence didn't just mean a flower not yet plucked. Her sanctuary .... In his mind the once-stalwart walls of outrage were crumbling."[39]

What he has taken is so much more than the value of the merchandise he has stolen — and he repents. Would anybody steal or harm another if we knew that we would feel the wound in our own experience? Could anybody resist repenting if we began to experience life through the eyes of another, particularly one who has less because of our more, or who hurts because of what we have said — no matter how righteous we may feel about it, and no matter how right we might genuinely be? Engagement with another is not a question of rightness but of understanding. When Jesus meets the Samaritan woman at the well [John 4], he teases her about her marital situation, but is still engaged, not judging but caring.

Repentance is the corrective, then, for what causes suffering; it is the sign that compassion has come to make a home in a person or group of persons. Repentance will not stop grief or illness or natural disaster, but it will affect the way we experience such losses and pains. We will cease to see ourselves as separate and begin to see ourselves as part of the whole, affecting and being affected as life twists and turns through the eternal moment. Each one of us comes to experience humility for our self-absorption, and awe at our power to effect change through the slightest action. Dr T. Crowley of the University of Guelph sees in the study of history the power of the individual to affect the course of events. No one is insignificant, although our role may ever be unknown, our participation hidden in history; but each of us carries a piece of this history. It is also true that each of us is the product of genetic variables, the time and conditions of our birth, the influences and experience that surround us. We cannot separate ourselves from the flow; we can only decide how we live in the stream of God's life as we witness it opening in this world.

Beyond Isolation

Repentance is the sign that a person has begun to forgive themselves for having had the knowledge of good and evil, but for still having lacked the maturity and wisdom to see from a broader perspective. The turning from one way of being to another way is an indication of deep inner change — a growing ability to see the self as an active and responsible participant in the universe. Perhaps the greatest barrier to true repentance and compassion is the curious combination of feeling powerless and isolated, capable of acting without reference to others, of living separately and independently. There is no such thing as a self-made person, no one who survives one day without the assistance of others, whether recognized or unknown.

"We are not alone," the United Church Creed says. But the truth is that we cannot be alone; to be alone we would have to exist in a different reality from the one we know. Why defend our isolation from the healing of community? To be alone suggests control over our lives, allows us to deny dissolution while pretending that we are the deities of our own lives. But the DNA of our bodies is shared by everything else that lives — trees, flowers, other creatures. Humanity is neither so different nor so separate from the rest of creation that we can sever our ties to the world, no matter how much we may abuse it and hold it hostage to our greed and fear.

For this reason, we cannot forgive others until we experience the depth of healing that is forgiveness of self. Forgiveness of self is the path to solidarity with others. In this experience, we see ourselves as needy, unfinished, dependent on the affirmation of others and the Divine; as children only beginning to take our first steps toward responsibility for, and active participation in, the unfolding of the universe. The most humbling reality is that the Divine has chosen humanity, despite our slow maturation, to be these participants, perhaps to be the creatures who bring all other creatures into the awareness of love and mercy. In his new book, *Spirit Matters*, Michael Lerner says,

> We can understand ourselves as one of the billion ways that Spirit has chosen to pour its love into existence. We are at once a manifestation of all the love of the universe, and an opportunity for the universe through us to manifest greater loving, cooperation, and harmony.... While we are here on earth, we have an incredible opportunity — to recognize and rejoice in the Unity of All being, to stand in

awe and wonder at the glory of all that is, and to bring forward as much consciousness, love, solidarity, creativity, sensitivity, and goodness as we can possibly manifest. Developing and refining this kind of consciousness is a central element of what it means to develop an inner life.[40]

HEALING

In accepting this role, we come to see that what is eternal is goodness and growth, and what is temporary is pain and loss and evil. If evil is ultimately the loser, then where should we place our energies? If pain is for the moment but, as Paul trusts, will be swallowed up in glory and joy, then we can say with him, "O death, where is thy sting? O grave, where is thy sting?" [1 Corinthians 15:55]. If loss has to do with how we view time, rather than how we view relationship, then our grief as it heals can be resolved into thankfulness for what we have had, rather than greed for what we think we have deserved. Repentance (turning) from our anger and bitterness and regret to the healing embrace of Christ's love places us within a universe of becoming, within a cosmos of healing change, within the promise of the vision of Julian of Norwich:

All this trusting in the real comfort is meant to be taken generally.... It is God's will. This word, 'You will not be overcome' was said very distinctly and firmly to give us comfort for whatever troubles may come. He did not say, 'You will never have a rough passage, you will never be over-strained, you will never feel uncomfortable', but he did say, 'You will never be overcome.' God wants us to pay attention to these words, so as to trust him always.... For he loves us, and delights in us; so he wills that we should love and delight in him in return, and trust him with all our strength. So all will be well.[41]

We have spoken frequently of healing as one of the signs of goodness, but what do we mean by healing? Healing is the result of true repentance. Healing comes as we accept the joys and challenges of the experiences as we choose them and as they come to us unbidden. Most of the popular understanding of healing has to do with cures, which may or may not be good in themselves. Healing differs from cure in that healing covers a wider expanse of the human soul, whereas cure affects only a localized problem.

There are several fallacies with the whole idea of a cure. The first is an unrealistic expectation that we are "owed" a long problem-free life. The second is that, for good people, all problems have directly applicable effective solutions. The third is that problems are errors or mistakes in the universe. The fourth is that these mistakes are either God's error or judgement, or our error, but someone is definitely to blame. Julian of Norwich notes the first fallacy about having a comfortable life. Indeed, most people who commit themselves to the spiritual life find that honesty, compassion, and vulnerability are antidotes to any blind comfort, even if their personal lives should escape the usual experiences of conflict and pain. Good people can be hurt, killed, oppressed, become ill, experience loss and betrayal. There is no seal that prevents good people from the pain of being alive in a world where all life is in flux and change. Expectations of spiritual vaccination are human constructions that serve either as social controls or to assuage the fear of being really alive and engaged.

If we want to fix the blame on God rather than ourselves, for a world that may not meet our expectations as a species, then we have to see ourselves as robotic rather than free; we are simply part of a dream that God had once and is now analyzing. In this scenario, everything that happens has a pre-existing meaning and purpose that presupposes a kind of sadistic and arbitrary judgement by God on an unsuspecting world. This idea of divinity has more to do with the Greek pantheon of anthropomorphic gods than the engaged, yet mysterious "Creator-who-is-becoming" of Moses and Jesus. There is no room for randomness in the configuration of reality that says it is all planned out. But in a configuration where healing rather than punishment is the dynamic, there is room for the randomness of life. There is opportunity to give meaning to our pain and loss, so that we may live with new strength and purpose. In the first case, we are victims of a providence that does not consult us, and in the second case, we are allies with an unfolding hope of radiant life. In a universe of potential rather than plan, there is also, tragically, room for us to hate and sabotage rather than promote life and healing.

For a cure, we are dependent upon the skill of others or the capriciousness of "God's will." In healing, we turn to find the Divine growing within us despite our illness or pain, and we turn to others in our life to restore relationship, to comfort and be comforted, to experience the possibility of new beginnings, to make connections that cannot be destroyed by our physical circumstances.

Healing can come only to people who open themselves to all the possibilities, and find the path to wholeness within and beyond their own consciousness. Others may or may not find cures, but they will not be healed of the deep wound that is our sense of isolation and loneliness in the face of an external universe, hostile at worst, indifferent at best. True healing is always characterized by a sense of peace, trust, good humour, and thankfulness for what has been given. People must come to see themselves as loveable and ultimately beloved; they must learn to understand themselves as part of the fabric of a beautiful and unfolding creation; they must grow to be curious about the greater mystery that is at the heart of the universe. As Christians, we come to know that God is expressed through revelation in the Anointed One, the Christ.

Healing does not have to wait for a crisis, of course. If religion is doing its job, its task is not really about ethics, because they are culturally and politically bound, but it is about healing. It is about helping people to open themselves in faith and trust, in hope and thanksgiving, to an awareness of life that transcends the limitations of our individual knowledge and existence. It invites people into a sense of cosmic belonging that is so radical that it changes the way we perceive everyone and everything. The cosmos, which is suffused with the radiance of God, and of which we are a permanent part whether living or dead, suggests to us that we can never be alone and will always be participating at a molecular level, a genetic level, a historical level, a cultural level, and, if we are believers, a spiritual level with Christ. Such awareness and participation is healing because it brings an end to ultimate suffering, which is our sense of betrayal before the reality of our mortality, and our sense of separation beginning with birth from our mother's womb. It is healing of the disjuncture that allowed us to become self-aware participants in the unfolding of the universe of which we are such a vital part.

Healing is ultimately a way of life. In the wedding ceremony, we say that marriage is a way of life that none should lightly undertake and all should reverence. Perhaps more to the point would be to say that healing is a way of life that all should reverence and none should lightly undertake, because it will affect not only our primary relationships but also how we interact in the community and, therefore, in the greater Life. Perhaps we need a different model of citizenship for children in school. Instead of asking them to obey or honour the dubious merits of political rulers and systems, we might ask children to commit themselves to a way of life that is healing of the world, respectful of others, and open to personal compassion and repentance.

The benefit of the healing lifestyle is that we can say with Paul: "Whether we live or whether we die, we are the Lord's," and we belong to this hope. For Christians, such hope is bound up in our call to follow Jesus, but for others the context of the healing life may be different. It seems to me that the qualities of person as self, as member of community, as citizen of the world, look remarkably similar from one form of spirituality to another. You will note that I am not talking about ethics but about attitudes, not about morality but about a spiritual perspective of the world and the universe that sees separation only as a stage of development rather than an end in itself, that sees all human societies as permeable and transient, that recognizes permanence only in the permutation of matter from one experience of itself to another. In *A Spirituality Named Compassion*, Matthew Fox defined compassion like this: "to be compassionate is to incorporate one's fullest energies with cosmic ones into the twin tasks of (1) relieving the pain of fellow creatures by way of justice-making, and (2) celebrating the existence, time and space that all creatures share as a gift from the only One who is fully Compassion. Compassion is our kinship with the universe and the universe's maker."[42]

To experience this compassion is to recognize the need for repentance and healing. From our awareness that our ego is not so much distinct as common to all other humans, that our urge to live and thrive is like the dandelions, the squirrels, the creatures of the deep sea, we can place ourselves with the Christ at the centre of the cross, the point of connection. From and through his great compassion, we receive courage to look at everything within us and everything beyond us. In this unity of consciousness, we are unafraid of our past and serene about our future. It is humility and repentance that teaches us to say "yes" with our hands outstretched in love and "no" to our fearful and warring egos. It is repentance that welcomes change as the blessing of the waters of baptism, the oil of peace and healing. It is the Holy within and beyond us that surrounds us with hope and vision, so that we may see more clearly. The mirror will be true for us; and we will be whole, and will abide in the heart of the Creator forever.

In repentance, compassion.

God of thunder and God of the silent waters, open us, move us,
teach us not to fear your judgement,
but welcome the change that brings us closer to you and to each other.
Broaden our roads, help us to welcome new companions,
let us see the face of your Beloved in those we meet.
Help us to feel your creative presence within the depths of our hearts.
Teach us not to fear the monsters, but to see the angels in the heights and in the depths.
In our living and in our dying, may your compassion be the meaning of our lives
and the nourishment we have shared with others.
Amen.

THE PARADOX OF THE ETERNAL

i look into the face of fear and pain,
it rolls over me, a tidal wave;
washed clean by the storm,
i look over my shoulder;
the pain and fear have passed,
the sunshine is blessing me again

As I thought through what I wanted to say in this book, I became aware that each idea kept turning in on itself. Whenever I examined one idea, it seemed attached to every other idea. Love and suffering, fear and sin, wisdom and change, healing and repentance, compassion and self-knowledge — all were held together in one pattern. Perhaps this one pattern comprises what we think of as the eternal mind of God, including the various bits and pieces of human and other life. Early in my thinking and praying, I became aware that I was spending time inside the labyrinth of paradox, where each corridor leads both ahead and back on itself. Although the pattern of paradox may seem like a maze, we can never really be lost because the way out and the way in are the same, through our bodies and our experiences.

When we speculate about the eternal, or about the big-picture view of life and the universe, we are arrested by the limits of our own intellect and our present store of knowledge, even though this store is more than any one person can assimilate. When we speak of the Divine outside strict and arbitrary limits imposed either by culture or interpretation, we must include seeming contradictions to almost everything that we can say. When we say that God is good, we also remember that, for many people, the experience of suffering has been understood to be as much the will of God as their redemption. I often hear people say that everything has a purpose, or that God would never send us more than we could bear. The story of Job in Hebrew scripture is a case in point.

Then Satan answered God, "Does Job fear God for nothing? Have you not put a fence around him and his house and all that he has, on every side? You have blessed the work of his hands, and his possessions have increased in the land. But stretch out your hand now, and touch all that he has, and he will curse you to your face." The Holy One said to Satan, "Very well, all that he has is in your power; only do not stretch out your hand against him!"

[Job 1:10–12]

Although this text suggests that God guesses what will happen, it also suggests an element of uncertainty. When we say that God is unchangeable, we acknowledge either that prayer is completely ineffectual or that, if God has a plan at all, it can be amended. If God's plan can be amended, then we must say that the divine mind can be changed and, therefore, that change is a quality of the eternal — a conclusion about God that continues to force itself upon us. When we say that God is the maker of heaven and earth, we must say that the only part of the universe we know well is the immediate environment of planet earth, and the only heaven we know is the one described by sages and mystics. What we know about God is either the product of our own projections, or a response to the image of the Divine within us, or a way of describing experiences that push us beyond language.

To consider the mystery that is the Divine in any way that hopes to expand our culturally biased pictures, we must accept paradox as a working reality of all that we know. To accept paradox as a quality of the Divine is to say that God is and is not, that everything we believe about God is and is not. One of the concerns for Christians is how this affects our Christology. Some see a threat in the possibility that the historical Jesus and the experience of the Risen Christ are expressions of the Divine designed and developed to fit Christian thinking, but not necessarily universal in their application. We can say that Jesus Christ is the only revelation for the church, but can we say that Holiness is not revealed in Buddhism, in Hinduism, in Sufism, in pantheism, and so on?

An example of the intentional application of paradox is to say that, for those who are called or discover themselves as Christians, Jesus Christ is the only Way, Truth, and Life. But this is not to say that such an experience of the Holy can be assumed for all other people on earth. We can say that, for those who "fit" the Christian model, there is no salvation outside the acceptance of Jesus Christ, but can we say this of others who have been shaped and moulded in different structures and perspectives? Thus, we can say that Jesus is the only child of God for Christians, that Jesus is the only path to God for Christians, that in Jesus the fullness of the Divine is revealed to Christians, and still allow that, for other people, there are different paths, different revelations, different dreams.

We can say that, whatever is the nature of the Divine, we believe that within it are held seeming contradictions of theology, ethics, spirituality, and lifestyle. If nothing that was made is separate from the Divine, and if everything that has come to be is also part of the Divine, then, in this fullness of being, we must allow for contradiction and the dynamic tension of perceived opposites. For Christians, the place of paradox is the centre of the cross, where we find the suffering Jesus and also the risen Christ. On the cross, we place our unswerving conviction that, for us, this Jesus, this Christ, is the Way, the Truth, and the Life, and that no one can understand Christian faith except through this mystery. What we also say is that, for others, the resolution of paradox does not exist on this cross, may not even require a god, may be equally full of truth, but it is not for us.

To extend this discussion, I would like to consider the contradictions and implications of some of the ideas that we have already considered, and also to place them in the frame of holy paradox that allows them and their opposites to exist together. We have said that change is the essential condition of the universe as we know it. We could say that God saw everything that was made and it was changing, just as easily as we can say that God saw everything and it was good. When death is no longer understood to be a threat but an unfolding of the power of life to transform and make new, then we no longer need an unchanging universe nor an immutable God. But is there anything that we want to continue to think about as eternally existing and as being eternally changeless?

This is a discussion of the essentials of reality. For Jews and Christians, the constant that occurs is the *chesed* of the Divine. This steadfast love is not so much fixed as it is encircling, spiralling back always to an original and indissoluble bond with creation. The stories and prophets tell us that, after each disaster or break in our relationship with God, the Divine "remembers" the original love for us and the earth, and "repents" of anger and judgement, turning to us with renewed concern and protection.

> The sun shall no longer be
> your light by day,
> nor for brightness shall the moon
> give light to you by night;
> but the Holy One will be your everlasting light,
> and your God will be your glory.
> Your sun shall no more go down,
> or your moon withdraw itself;
> for the Holy One will be your everlasting light,
> and your days of mourning shall be ended.
> Your people shall all be righteous;
> they shall possess the land forever.
> They are the shoot that I planted, the work of my hands,
> so that I might be glorified.
> The least of them shall become a clan,
> and the smallest one a mighty nation;
> I am the Holy One;
> in its time I will accomplish it quickly.
> [Isaiah 60:19–22]

We understand, then, that nothing can separate us from the Holy Love of God, which may not always be gentle or even kind by human standards, but is constant in that it always returns to its point of original holiness and blessing. If everything spirals back into God's love, then it would seem that any evil we intend and act out is without much point. We might remember Paul's vision on the road to Damascus, when he learns that his "crimes" will only increase his own torment rather than bring him peace or satisfaction [Acts 9:1–9]. For the people of Hebrew and Christian scripture, then, the eternal love of God is a relative constant — relative in that it remains in orbit with human experience, constant in that it always returns to the still point of the primary impulse for creation.

The other thing we can say is that reality is about ongoing creation and revelation. This is a tough point for those who cling to a single act of creation rather than an unfolding process in which creatures and species have lifespans and ages, and then disappear to give way to new forms and new species. Humans are fearful of this process, and so we attempt to cling to all the stages of evolution at the same time. Hence we have the movies about time travel in the Star Trek future, or the era of dinosaurs intruding on the present, or a frozen human being revivified so that all ages can coexist.

We do not like the idea that, as a species, we may also have a limited lifespan that is not simply threatened by large cosmic events, but is in fact our natural process of evolution and change. Although Paul speaks of the resurrection as being a major shift — in that we will inherit a materially different kind of body — Christians rapidly reinvented a resurrection in which we have the same bodies and behave in a very similar way, just without death this time. I am amazed at how much we cling to ideas about this life, not because it is necessarily so satisfying, but because it is what we know. I would invite people to think about an eternity of sameness, and then to consider whether we really want change to disappear from the experience of being alive.

Not only is creation changing and evolving or devolving, depending on perspective, but so is the revelation of who is in the universe and what is our relationship to the Creator. This is an equally sore point for those who would like revelation to have been completed during the time of the resurrection appearances of the Anointed One — completion being marked by his ascension into a literal heaven. Then the church could remain on earth as keeper of the tradition, an unchanging, completely fulfilled revelation, which we might struggle to understand but which is complete in itself. I believe this is a dead end for serious thinkers, who can easily spot the problems with such a tidy plot that seems in almost direct contradiction to the Pentecost experience. And yet, perhaps in one possible reality, there was a plan and we followed it. In this reality, the plot clearly was adjusted as the church became the world of empire and the world became a vehicle for state religion. The irony of the Jewish peasant rebel agenda serving the armies of one type of tyrant or another is either shocking or tragic.

Another way of thinking about the unfolding history of the world is to acknowledge that absolutely nothing is finished. Not only is our knowledge partial, but existence itself is partial because the last chapter has yet to be written. If there is a master plan, then it is not yet fully revealed. More likely, if there is no plan, then we do not yet perceive how we are to function in developing reality and participating in the cosmos. We have only begun to think about what it means to be in relationship with each other. Jesus taught us that, as we learned to love one another, to shelter one another, to discover the power of vulnerability, the unity in the dismemberment of the cross, then we would come to know something about the Divine. We would begin to be in mutual relationship with the Holy One, and it would be possible to see ourselves and our place in the universe more clearly. If what we are seeking is the way to God — which is to say to wholeness, to holiness, through repentance and healing — then we want to touch the goodness that lies within our cells, the goodness that broods over the universe, the goodness that begins and ends everything with blessing and the power of love.

How, then, do we define what is good? The creation story tells us that essentially everything is good; that at the moment of beginning everything is good. Everything comes from goodness and has goodness as its originating spark. Everything is motivated by goodness and resolves in goodness. But when we speak ontologically, we are able to say that whatever is close to the source of being, the originating principle, is good. Not because of what it is or is not doing, or what it is or is not believing, but because of its state of being alive. At heart, then, everything is good because at one moment everything was in the state of coming into existence. If most things attempt to return to their original nature, then we can say that everything is groaning to be born again, struggling to return to another state of coming into being. Everything wants to change, everything wants to be born, everything wants to be complete, everything wants to be at that original centre of existence. But we know that when we return to the eternal river, we will not be what we were but a new creation, something different, as all that we have been is blended into the new creation. We shall be conscious and lovingly, passionately, aware of being part of all that is.

If good is the ontological nature of the universe, then matter, as it changes and flows into and out of different forms of itself, expresses the goodness of a new creation. The particular gift for humans is to be conscious, to be aware of the process of holiness birthing us, filling us, flowing through us, breaking us, and remaking us. It can destroy the tyranny of our demanding egos and our defiant need to be autonomous, but it fulfills our desperate need to belong. It acknowledges the value of the forms we take as we participate with God in the unfolding of the universe. Perhaps one day we will stand at a crest of human development and these thoughts will appear as quaint ideas of a primitive time, but until then I am going to gamble on a universe that is fully inhabited by holiness, that is the child of holiness, that is the journey of holiness, that is the Alpha and Omega that births change and compassion.

I remain a Christian because for me the story of Jesus, his faith and teachings, are the Way, the Truth, and the Life. For me, Christianity is essentially about these truths. Everything begins and ends in goodness. In the growth of wisdom, everything we know is changed. Change causes us to suffer, and our suffering reunites us with our sense of belonging, of wholeness. The remedy for isolation is compassion, which we learn through repentance as we discover and accept ourselves as monsters and angels. Paradox is the defining principle of reality.

And finally, Jesus is the one who has walked this road before, who was able to find a pathway through distraction and fear and his own suffering. Jesus was able to stand in solidarity with everyone who suffers, to sit at table with monsters and other sinners, was able to love those whom he met. Jesus knew a loving God of goodness and mercy, a God who cared about all the little ones and not much about structures and forms and rules and labels. I do not care whether or not he walked on water or did tricks with wine. I have little interest in his parentage and whether it matters how much he owed to being divine and how much his DNA looked like mine.

What I really care about is learning how he could love so much that people felt cared about beyond his death, beyond his humiliation. What matters to me is his strength of spirit that can reach out to me 2003 years beyond his death to claim me, a mixture of monster and angel, for the work of love. When we speak about relationship, we re-member ourselves in the context of that relationship. When we speak about our connection to the Holy One, we re-member that we, the partial ones, are already whole and fulfilled in our beginning and our ending. For love we walk the labyrinth of possibility where anything is possible and yet all things already exist in love and goodness. We are contained within the walls of this goodness. But within these walls, within this garden that is old and new, we recreate ourselves, and we learn and change and grow until this garden is full and we discover we are a star. And another star explodes into being, and a new beginning is born.

SPIRITUAL EXERCISES

B eing faithful to spiritual growth and new understanding demands that we find a way to integrate learnings and challenges. You may want to spend some time with any new thoughts or understandings that arise for you as you read this book. Each chapter ends with a prayer, and below are some spiritual exercises. I hope that these may be helpful in bringing any moments of new understanding within.

Each exercise offers a brief reflection and a litany of questions to inspire you to journal or quietly ponder the depths of your understanding. You might light a candle, or use a special journal, or choose a particular time of day to spend in reflection. You may work with an exercise during the same period of time that you read a particular chapter, or you may take as long as the Spirit guides you. Keep your reflections close to your heart each day and allow them to stir in your consciousness. Spend time with your spirit, your heart, your faith. If you encounter either difficult or inspiring ideas, share them with someone you trust. Offer your thoughts to the Holy One, and trust in the Spirit of Transformation.

IN ALL THINGS, GOODNESS

This moment is a new beginning. Every moment is a new beginning. Life is always just beginning. You are just beginning, no matter how old or young you may be. Think about how cellular history has stretched for aeons to make just you, no one like you ever before or to follow. You are a unique and special gift of God to the world, and the world is God's gift to you. You are good because what you are made of had its origins in God. No matter what you have done, no matter what has happened to you, nothing can touch that spark at the centre of your soul that began its travel outward from the Holy One.

- Write down four things that you have witnessed today that are good, whether they are glimpses of nature, actions of others, or experiences of beauty or mercy.

- Write down four things that you have done in your life that are signs of your own goodness.

Take time to be still. Feel the presence of God surrounding you, filling you with delight and compassion. In this light and love, you are resting for all eternity. This truth is for you to cherish and to hold like a lantern when you are afraid of the dark, and like a birthday-cake candle when you are rejoicing. This is the truth: that you are part of the Holy One; you are God's child and you are good; you are becoming whole and holy.

Gracious Creator, who lights the stars and sweeps the world with your breath, help us to experience your pervasive goodness in all that we see and all that we do. Teach us to view the world with your compassion, and your wisdom so that we may grow closer in trust of you and in love for others.

In Change, Wisdom

Wisdom calls to people everywhere to be bold in asking questions, and to mistrust easy answers. Wisdom calls us to look deeper, investigate more fully, use our intuition, our intellect, our knowledge, our hearts to learn about ourselves and our world. Wisdom teaches us to learn without doing harm, to recreate our environment without damaging the garden that God has made. The human heart is one of God's gardens. Every garden is in danger until we learn to cherish this first garden of our knowing.

- What do you need to know to be satisfied about your life? What will this knowledge bring you? Will you be different for this knowing? Will you be any more or less a child of God?

- What do you need to learn so that your knowledge can be tested and refined? How do you need to change in order to believe in God's love and mercy?

Listen for Wisdom calling in your heart. Think about the questions. The ones to which you can respond immediately are merely the beginning. Let the Spirit of inquiry and contemplation take you to the wilderness, to hear the voice of the Holy One calling your name and drawing a path you might choose.

God of desert and oasis, God of rocky mountains and cool streams, engage our hearts and minds in learning about ourselves, so that we may experience you more deeply and other people more clearly. Teach us not to fear the silence when we cannot hear your voice, or the whirlwind when you draw us into your reality. Encourage us to be faithful courageous pilgrims, that as we come to know you more nearly, we may love more graciously and more generously.

In Suffering, Wholeness

Suffering is the time spent alone with our fears, our sense of abandonment. Wholeness is the awareness that we are connected to everything that is and has been. Both of these experiences are holy and full of the Spirit's power to transform our lives.

- If Jesus were to visit you today, what experience of suffering would you place on the cross where he stands and which he circumnavigates as he heals us? Where would you place your suffering — at the centre, at the edges, on an arm of the cross?

- What would it mean for you to add your suffering to the suffering of the world? What do you hold back from healing? What will you lose, and what do you fear will be expected of you?

Sit facing a door. Think about how little separates you from the whole world, and yet how the door restrains other life from entering, and how much it would cost you to break through to the other side. What does your door look like?

Think about the door you see. Think about the door you would like to see. What kind of doorway could connect you with the world and yet provide a place for you to contemplate the suffering of the world?

> Merciful God, you weep when we weep and you rage at injustice. Yet even so, you are the God of forgiveness and steadfast love. Help us to see the universe unfolding in love despite the immaturity of us, your people.

In Repentance, Compassion

There are many stories of monsters who were tamed by love. Jesus has taught us that no weapon can protect us from monsters. There is only one way to deal with a monster, and that is with compassion. We do not always use our inner angels to love our inner monsters. Sometimes we think we are being angelic when really we are being self-righteous, condescending, or condemnatory. Angels must be compassionate; monsters must learn patience.

- What monsters hide within you? Have you ever shown them to anyone?

- What kind of nurture does a monster need? What kind of love do you need, so that you will not be afraid of yourself?

Draw or describe your inner monsters and angels. If you brought them together, what kind of reception would you have: a dinner party? a war? a business meeting? a church service? What do your angels and monsters need for a better way to live together? How can this imaginary interaction tell you something about how our own humility can change the world around us?

> Compassionate God, in whom is our dream of heaven and the peaceful dream of earth, help us to love ourselves and to forgive ourselves, so that we can love and forgive our neighbours and those whom we do not want to know. Break us and heal us, so that we may be strengthened by the fire of your love, and tempered by the heat of your compassion. In the name of Jesus, who lived in the full experience of Love, inspire our hearts with his passion and his faith in you.

Endnotes

1. In the discussion between Matthew Fox and Rupert Sheldrake on transcendence, Fox makes the reference to Buckminster Fuller. For Fox, it means that transcendence is essentially about "surprise"; that is, the Spirit cannot be defined by human perception of reality, or by the limitations of our knowledge. Fox adds that, while there is no up or down in a curved universe, there is only "in and out." I would further suggest that "in and out" are also only a question of perception rather than a definable reality. Who is in and who is out? What is in the universe and what is outside it? Who has a share in salvation and who doesn't? These kinds of questions are ceasing to have validity as we are growing into new understanding of how the cosmos is formed. *From Natural Grace: Dialogues on Creation, Darkness, and the Soul in Spirituality and Science,* by Matthew Fox and Rupert Sheldrake (New York: Doubleday Dell Publishing Company, 1996), p. 38.

2. Richard Holloway, the former Primus of the Episcopal Church of Scotland, in *Dancing on the Edge,* says, "We have to look steadily and without fear at the new reality that

confronts us, knowing that it could be a gift from the God who is already ahead of us.... We have to find the courage to say yes to the truth, blindly following the paradox that Christ is truth before he is Christ, and in following truth we will fall, at last, into his arms" (London: HarperCollins, 1997), p. 195.

3. In *Can We Be Good without God? Behaviour, Belonging, and the Need to Believe,* Robert Buckman develops an argument against religion as an ethical guideline. I would suggest that he is quite correct, in that ethical behaviour both affects and is affected by cultural and historical considerations. Religion can be a powerful tool in influencing people for better or worse. I will discuss goodness as a quality of existence rather than as a particular ethic or cultural expectation (Toronto: Penguin Books, 2001).

4. Frederick Buechner, *The Longing for Home: Recollections and Reflections* (New York: HarperCollins Publishers, 1996), p. 126, 129–130.

5. The Judaeo-Christian religio-cultural history is only one global artefact, and if we had enough time, we would find within this particular history numerous variations, translations, segments lost or rewritten to suit different times and purposes. Many other cultures have equally valuable and equally insightful stories of how people make meaning of both joy and suffering within the context of the brevity of human life.

6. Although everyone probably knows by now that "Adam" is not a proper name but a common noun meaning "creature of clay" (human/adam, soil/adamah), I hear a persistent need to think of this passage as an event involving two individuals, named Adam and Eve. See *The Five Books of Moses: A New Translation with Introductions,* with Commentary and Notes by Everett Fox (New York: Schocken Books Inc., 1995).

7. See *The Other Bible,* ed. Willis Barnstone, "The War of the Sons of Light with the Sons of Darkness" (San Francisco: Harper & Row, 1984). Although Christianity has struggled with the dualism so obviously presented here: light/dark, enemy/ally, cursed/blessed, and so on, a cursory look at our hymns and many of our prayers demonstrates how caught up we still are in the world of either/or. See also Elaine Pagels, *The Origin of Satan* (New York: Vintage Books, Random House, 1995).

8, 9. Barbara G. Walker, *The Woman's Encyclopedia of Myths and Secrets* (San Francisco: Harper & Row, 1983), p. 905.

10. See Elaine Pagels, *The Origin of Satan,* p. 39: "In the Hebrew Bible, as in mainstream Judaism to this day, Satan never appears as Western Christendom has come to know him.... As he first appears in the Hebrew Bible, Satan is not necessarily evil, much less opposed to God. On the contrary, he appears ... as one of God's obedient servants.... In biblical sources, the Hebrew term 'satan' de-

scribes an adversarial role. It is not the name of a particular character."

11. Elaine Pagels, *Adam, Eve and the Serpent* (New York: Random House, 1988), p. 69.

12. John Milton, *Paradise Lost, Book XII,* contains a rationale for the necessity of "Adam's" disobedience: that from these first parents would ultimately come a more glorious picture of God and eternal life for humanity through the Christ. I have never found this a comforting or reassuring concept, but Milton's poetry is grand.

13. Typology is biblical interpretation derived from the Greek, *typos,* meaning a pattern. As used by Paul, it suggests that the incarnate weakness of Adam prefigures the incarnate perfection of Christ.

14. Thomas Merton, *Seeds of Contemplation* (Wheathampstead, U.K.: Anthony Clarke Books, 1961), p. 230: "For the world and time are the dance of the Lord in emptiness. The silence of the spheres is the music of a wedding feast.... We are invited to forget ourselves on purpose, cast our awful solemnity to the winds and join in the general dance."

15. Elie Wiesel, *From the Kingdom of Memory: Reminiscences* (New York: Schocken Books, 1990), p. 160.

16. Elie Wiesel, *From the Kingdom of Memory*, p. 185. Wiesel makes several important conclusions for the argument of this chapter: (1) The harm we cause ultimately rebounds, indeed "unto the third and fourth generation"; (2) In order to cause such harm, we need to "depersonalize" the victims, and in so doing, we ourselves are depersonalized.

17. Heisenberg's principle of uncertainty states that it is impossible to determine at the same time the exact speed and position of a particle, and the smaller the particle, the greater the uncertainty. The relative size of the "particle" depends on perspective, of course. Thus, from a cosmic perspective, we "human germs" are extremely unpredictable, which is perhaps why the Creator is interested in us. If the Creator is both the sum of all the created parts and more than this as well, then all these random activities must produce a factor of unpredictability in the Divine.

18. Susan Griffin, *Woman and Nature: The Roaring Inside Her*, "The Possible" (New York: Perennial Library, Harper & Row Publishers, 1978), pp. 191–192.

19. Deuteronomy 30:19: "I call heaven and earth to witness against you this day that I have set before you life and death, blessings and curses. Choose life so that you and your descendants may live."

20. See J. Coert Rylaarsdam, *Revelation in Jewish Wisdom Literature* (Chicago: University of Chicago Press, 1946), chapter 1.

21. See R.B.Y. Scott, *The Way of Wisdom in the Old Testament* (New York: MacMillan Publishing Co. Inc., 1971), p. 46.

22. See Gabriele Boccaccini, *Middle Judaism: Jewish Thought 300 B.C.E. to 200 C.E.* (Minneapolis: Fortress Press, 1991), especially chapter 3, in which he discusses how Sirach attempted to restore a balance in the face of a less optimistic view of the law and the covenant.

23. R.B.Y. Scott, *The Way of Wisdom*, p. 48.

24. Elaine Pagels, *The Gnostic Gospels* (New York: Vintage Books, Random House, 1981), pp. 131–32, 137–38.

25. See Mark 14:29 and 66–72.

26. Elisabeth Schussler Fiorenza, *Bread Not Stone: The Challenge of Feminist Biblical Interpretation* (Boston: Beacon Press, 1984), p. 15: "A feminist critical interpretation begins with a hermeneutics of suspicion, rather than a hermeneutics of consent and affirmation. It develops a hermeneutics of proclamation rather than a hermeneutics of historical factualness…. It develops a hermeneutics of remembrance that moves from biblical texts about women to the reconstruction of women's history. Finally, this model moves from a hermeneutics of disinterested

distance to hermeneutics of creative actualization that involves the church of women in the imaginative articulation of women's biblical story and its ongoing history and community." I would suggest that, while this is an ongoing task for women in the church, we now know that it is also a task for the whole church: to question what we have received, to analyze and deconstruct the material, to remember the stories in new ways, and to make this sense of the living Word of the Holy One part of our understanding of a church that itself lives in the present, believes through contemporary knowledge, and functions as community that is not bound by rules but encouraged by possibility.

27. Barbara G. Walker, *The Woman's Encyclopedia of Myths and Secrets,* p. 352. See her comparison of the chalice with the Holy Grail.

28. John Shelby Spong, *Liberating the Gospels: Reading the Bible with Jewish Eyes* (San Francisco: Harper, 1996): Spong's perspective on the gospels as liturgical books meant to follow the seasonal reading of Torah is worth noting here. As well, others have also commented on how this episode both teaches about the eucharist and describes a model for eucharist.

29. Elaine Scarry, *The Body in Pain: The Making and Unmaking of the World* (New York and Oxford: Oxford University Press, 1985), p. 4.

30. Dietrich Bonhoeffer, *Life Together* (San Francisco: Harper, 1993), p. 100.

31. Thomas Merton, *Love and Living*, "Seven Words" (San Diego, New York, London: Harvard/HBJ Book, Harcourt Brace Jovanovich Publishers, 1985), p. 102.

32. Elaine Scarry, *The Body in Pain*, p. 214.

33. Doing a casual piece of completely unsubstantiated research, I have noted that the most popular television shows among people I know are either hospital dramas or law enforcement shows involving dangerous criminals. They are essentially about the power to destroy or restore life, human hubris at an unsophisticated level.

34. Roger Bacon (1220–1292), a Franciscan philosopher who believed that scientific experimentation would reveal more about God. For a modern approach, see also John M. Templeton and Robert L. Herrmann, *The God Who Would Be Known: Revelations of the Divine in Contemporary Science* (San Francisco: Harper & Row, Publishers, 1989). John Polkinghorne, *Belief in God in an Age of Science* (New Haven: Yale University Press, 1998), p. 24: "I am a passionate believer in the unity of knowledge and I believe that those who are truly seeking an understanding through and through, and who will not settle for a facile and premature conclusion to that search, are seeking God, whether they acknowledge that quest or not."

35. Thomas Merton, *Love and Living*, p. 22.

36. See John Meier's discussion of Jesus and John the Baptist in *A Marginalized Jew (Rethinking the Historical Jesus)* vol. 2 (New York: Doubleday, 1994), chapter 13, especially p. 124.

37. Susan Griffin, *The Eros of Everyday Life: Essays on Ecology, Gender and Society* (New York: Doubleday Dell Publishing Group Inc., 1995), pp. 152–153.

38. Jorge Luis Borges, "Dreamtigers" *Paradiso* XXXL, 108, trans. Mildred Boyer and Harold Morland (New York: E.P. Dutton & Co. Inc., 1970), p. 43.

39. Steven Erikson, *Gardens of the Moon* (Great Britain: Bantam Books, 1999), p. 234.

40. Michael Lerner, *Spirit Matters,* from *Tikkun,* Volume 15, Number 3 (Charlottesville, VA: Hampton Roads, 2000), p. 34.

41. Julian of Norwich, *Revelations of Divine Love,* trans. Clifton Wolters (London: Penguin Classics, 1966), p. 185.

42. Matthew Fox, *A Spirituality Named Compassion and the Healing of the Global Village, Humpty Dumpty and Us* (Minneapolis: Winston Press, 1979), p. 34.

ABC Publishing
ANGLICAN BOOK CENTRE

Mansions of the Spirit
The Gospel in a Multi-Faith World
Michael Ingham
Michael Ingham explores the place of Christianity among
world religions and offers a way forward — grounded
openness, a deep personal commitment to Christ that can
open Christians to the grace of God in other great spiritual
traditions.
1-55126-185-5 $18.95

Discerning the Word
The Bible and Homosexuality in Anglican Debate
Paul Gibson
Focusing on the 1998 Lambeth Conference resolutions on
scripture and sexuality, Paul Gibson examines the way cultural norms influence our understanding of biblical authority.
He issues a challenge to the church, and proposes a way forward that honours scripture, tradition, and our evolving
culture.
1-55126-320-3 $14.95

All Who Minister
New Ways of Serving God's People
Maylanne Maybee, editor
These first-hand stories from the frontiers of alternative ministry, and ground-breaking articles on the theology of ministry, offer inspiring models and rationales for all who minister — whether in a venerable tradition or on the forefront of change. Exciting and creative!
1-55126-341-6 $24.95

Seeking the Seekers
Serving the Hidden Spiritual Quest
Paul MacLean and Michael Thompson
Using an approach that congregations can readily follow, the authors develop practical and effective strategies to reconnect with people's daily lives and inject new relevance into the church's mission.
1-55126-308-4 $16.95

Alive Again
Recession and Recovery in the Churches
Reginald Stackhouse
In this fascinating study of "growth churches" across Canada, Stackhouse recounts real stories about real churches he has visited and considers the reasons for their exceptional growth.
1-55126-257-6 $16.95

The Challenge of Tradition
Discerning the Future of Anglicanism
John Simons, editor
Fresh perspectives on a wide range of hotly debated issues —
feminism, names of God, authority of scripture, liturgical
renewal, social gospel, evangelism, mission, homosexuality, and
tolerance. Includes a process for Bible study and reflection.
1-55126-163-4 $18.95

Available from your local bookstore or

Anglican Book Centre
(416) 924-1332
toll-free 1-800-268-1168
email: abc@national.anglican.ca
Internet: www.abcpublishing.com